SHADE-TREES IN TOWNS AND CITIES

STREET OF PIN OAKS: Eppirt Street, East Orange, N. J., Planted by the Shade-Tree Commission in April, 1905. View taken, August, 1910.

SHADE-TREES IN TOWNS AND CITIES

THEIR SELECTION, PLANTING, AND CARE AS APPLIED
TO THE ART OF STREET DECORATION; THEIR
DISEASES AND REMEDIES; THEIR MUNI-
CIPAL CONTROL AND SUPERVISION

BY

WILLIAM SOLOTAROFF, B.S.

SECRETARY AND SUPERINTENDENT OF THE SHADE-TREE
COMMISSION OF EAST ORANGE, N. J

TOTAL ISSUE, FOUR THOUSAND

NEW YORK
JOHN WILEY & SONS
LONDON: CHAPMAN & HALL, LIMITED

12/20

PRESS OF
BRAUNWORTH & CO.
BOOK MANUFACTURERS
BROOKLYN, N. Y.

TO EVERY TOWN

AND CITY DWELLER

THIS BOOK

IS EARNESTLY DEDICATED

PREFACE

DURING the last few years there has been a remarkable growth of interest in the planting of trees for ornament and shade. In an editorial of February 10, 1909, the *Savannah News* remarked: "The increasing interest in shade-trees in practically all of the cities of the country is worthy of more than a passing notice. This interest seems to be keeping abreast of the sanitary reforms that are being inaugurated. While it isn't stated that there is a connection between tree-planting and hygienic reforms, there is no doubt that shade-trees contribute to the healthfulness of a city. . . . . The shade-trees have a restful effect, because making homes more attractive. That which tends to give rest and pleasure must also contribute to healthfulness."

The awakening of interest in tree-planting has been followed by the development of the movement for shade-tree departments in towns and cities. The Shade-Tree Commission of East Orange, N. J., organized in the spring of 1904, was the third in the State. There are now thirty-one towns and cities in New Jersey that have such departments. The work of the Shade-Tree Commissions, of Newark and East Orange especially, has proved very successful, and during the last few years there have come to these departments hundreds of requests from different parts of the country for information regarding methods of work and forms of organization. The cities of New Jersey may have inspired others. In 1907, Pennsylvania passed a shade-tree

law modeled after the New Jersey statute. Within the last
three or four years the cities of Buffalo, St. Louis, Chicago,
New Orleans, and Pittsburg have established shade-tree
departments.

The *Harrisburg Patriot,* in an editorial, January 13, 1909,
said: "We do not see how any one . . . . can doubt the
wisdom of a speedy acceptance of the law of 1907 authori-
zing the placing of all shade-trees in charge of a Shade-Tree
Commission. The fine results obtained in East Orange
and elsewhere . . . . could never have been obtained by
individual effort at any outlay of money. But it has been
demonstrated in East Orange that it is less expensive to
get and maintain a splendid, harmonious, and beautiful
system of shade-trees, than it is to have such a haphazard
arrangement as prevails in most cities where great possibilities are ruined sometimes through indifference and
inattention, but more often through ignorance."

To supply the needs of the growing demand for information regarding the planting, care, and control of shade-trees
in towns and cities is the aim of this book. It is the result
of the study of shade-trees in a great many towns and
cities of the country and experience gained in the administration of the work of the East Orange Shade-Tree
Commission since its organization. While in the preparation of the book the author has used for reference the
bulletins of agricultural experiment stations, treating of
some phases of the subject, the material has to him taken
on a living form through actual practise. The principles
laid down are of general application, and it is the writer's
hope that the book may prove helpful in spreading the tree-
planting movement throughout the United States.

With the increase of the number of shade-tree departments has grown the demand for trained men to take charge of the work, and as a result many forest schools are introducing courses in the care of trees. The writer has tried to shape and present the material in such a way as to make the book useful to the private owner of trees, to those endeavoring to establish municipal tree departments, and to those in charge of the work of such departments.

The book treats particularly of the planting and care of street-trees. As in this work, however, the most adverse conditions for tree growth have to be overcome, the problem is considered from the severest standpoint; and the book, therefore, covers the planting and care of shade and ornamental trees in state and county roads, public parks, private grounds, and other places. Some of the methods, such as pruning and tree surgery, apply to fruit-trees as well.

The writer wishes to acknowledge his gratitude to the members of the East Orange Shade-Tree Commission for their encouragement in the preparation of this work. All references to the methods of tree-planting in the city of Washington are the result of personal visits and study and information kindly furnished by Mr. Trueman Lanham, Superintendent of the Trees and Parkings Division of the District of Columbia, whose courtesy has been very much appreciated. Authorities for reference to methods used in the city of Paris have been correspondence with the Prefect of the Seine, who has charge of the street-trees of Paris, and *Les Arbres de la Ville de Paris,* by A. Chargueraud. Acknowledgment is due to Dr. N. L. Britton, Director-in-Chief of the New York Botanical Garden, for looking over the manuscript of Chapter III.; to Mr. George B. Sudworth, Dendrologist, United States Forest Service, for looking over the manuscript of the first half of the book; to Dr. W. A.

Murrill, First Assistant of the New York Botanical Garden, for suggestions as to the method of treatment of the part of the book on fungous diseases and for naming some species of fungi; and to Mr. Irving T. Guild, Secretary of the Massachusetts Forestry Association for furnishing information regarding the shade-tree laws of Massachusetts. The author also wishes to remember the many kindnesses of Dr. James P. Haney, of the New York City Department of Education, who first suggested to him the idea of writing the book.

All the photographs and sketches for the illustrations are by the author, with the exception, of Plate 24, Fig. 4; Plate 41, Fig. 4; and Plate 42, Fig. 5. The making of the photographs extended over a period of more than five years. Those elucidating methods of work were taken during operations in East Orange.

WILLIAM SOLOTAROFF.

EAST ORANGE, N. J., January, 1911.

CONTENTS

xi

LIST OF ILLUSTRATIONS

PLATES

xv

FIGURES

SHADE-TREES IN TOWNS AND CITIES

CHAPTER I

TREES IN THE LIFE OF A CITY

It is a well-known fact that cities are founded in certain particular localities on account of some commercial incentive. Any situation offering special advantages as a place where business men may conveniently meet, or commodities may be cheaply manufactured or easily exchanged, is likely to be occupied by a town or city. Places that are near to sources of natural wealth, at the mouths of navigable rivers, at falls or rapids of streams or at large and deep harbors, are sites favorable for the location of large cities.

Whatever the reason may be that induces people to settle in a certain place, their first desire is to build shelters and homes in which to live. With this thought in mind, every natural feature of the land is swept away to make room for the city. As it grows there is an addition of square block to square block, and a plan of the resulting city looks like a huge checkerboard.

Such, briefly, has been the history of the development of most of our cities. When this country was first settled the forest was regarded as an enemy to be vanquished rather than as a friend to be protected. The country seemed so vast and the natural resources so limitless that no one ever

1

supposed there would come a time when we should be in danger of losing our natural heritage. When cities were built there was no attempt, in most cases, to set aside certain areas for park purposes or to conserve portions of the natural forests as playgrounds for the people. The cities of to-day show the lack of foresight of the original builders. At a meeting for the discussion of tree-planting, held in Fullerton Hall, Chicago, on January 31, 1909, Mr. Franklin Mac-Veagh, who presided, said that when he first saw Chicago it was a tree city. The trees were many and fine. Splendid trees were cut down over large areas where the city now stands. This statement would apply equally as well not only to Chicago but to a great many other cities.

With the development of society, acquisition of wealth, and increased culture through education and travel, there has come the recognition that cities must not only be the sites of manufacture and commerce, but attractive places in which one would enjoy to live. This spirit for betterment is finding expression in a great many ways. There are efforts to secure clean streets, to inaugurate sanitary reforms, to build better dwellings, and to improve transportation facilities. The acquirement of land for parks and playgrounds is becoming a necessity, and the importance of comprehensive city planning is being felt.

One of the material aids to the health and attractiveness of cities and towns is trees, and the increasing interest in shade-trees in practically all of the cities of the country is a proof that their value is being recognized. The cultivation of trees in cities is beneficial in many ways. In the realization of the City Beautiful shade-trees play a very important part. No city in America possesses such avenues of fine shade-trees as the city of Washington. While visitors admire the fine public buildings, every one will admit that the chief attractions of Washington are the beautiful avenues of shade-trees, which make it one magnificent park.

The eighty-six thousand trees of the city of Paris constitute one of its glories. They are not only the most potent factor of the city's beauty, but also illustrate most strikingly the possibilities of cultivating a large variety of trees in streets and public places of large cities under adverse conditions. The Prefect of the Department of the Seine, who has jurisdiction over the trees of Paris, writes me that the soil along the Paris streets is generally very poor. That the trees of that city succeed is largely due to the great care taken in setting them out and maintaining them.

In the more recently developed suburban towns, where property is high, the houses are built near together and close to the street-line, so that there is not much of front lawn. On such streets the uniform planting of trees relieves the harshness of the perspective of a row of bare houses. Besides softening the hard lines of buildings, the trees, because of their beauty, are a continuous source of pleasure. They have a restful effect and possess an unceasing interest at all seasons of the year. In the winter, we can study their outlines, branching, bark, and buds. In the spring, we look forward to the appearance of the tree flowers. In the summer, the trees are in the full majesty of their beauty. In the fall, before they lose their leaves, the trees attract our attention by the brilliant coloring of their autumn livery.

From the viewpoint of health, we need but recall a few well-known facts. Trees help to purify the air by absorbing the carbonic-acid gas that is exhaled by man, and giving back the pure oxygen he needs. The animal and the vegetable world therefore complement each other, and one furnishes the conditions and forces by which the other maintains life and health. Trees also help to modify the temperature of our streets, and add to the comfort of the residents. The normal heat of summer is still further intensified in cities by the reflections from the pavements and the buildings. Besides cutting off the direct and the reflected rays of the sun, foliage exercises a marked effect on the temperature by evaporating large quantities of water from its surface, and the reduction of the temperature so resulting is greatest on dry, hot days when relief is much needed.

The appraisal of the tree as a sanitary factor in the life of the city was confirmed by the Commissioner of Health of the city of New York, who, in 1872, reported on the causes of the high death-rate during the summer months in the city of New York. The chief cause was determined to be the excessive heat which characterized those months.[1] It was recommended in the report to the Board of Health that legislation be secured empowering and requiring the Department of Parks to plant and cultivate trees in all of the streets, avenues, and public places in the city. The value of trees to the health of a city was further emphasized by the passage of the following resolution by the New York County Medical Society:

"Resolved, that one of the most effective means for mitigating the intense heat of the summer months and diminishing the death-rate among children is the cultivation of an adequate number of trees in the streets."

The economic value of shade-trees is inestimable. They add to the value of real estate, and are among the first

[1] "Vegetation a Remedy for the Summer Heat of Cities," by Stephen Smith, M.D., LL.D., *Popular Science Monthly,* February, 1899.

things that impress a stranger as to whether a city is or is not a good place to live in. Real-estate people are aware that beautiful trees will increase the value of their property and draw men and money to a city. Consequently we find that in the majority of cases of modern land development, trees are set out as soon as the streets are opened. It is unfortunate at such times that the choice of species is not always wise; but the planting serves to illustrate the fact that the trees are recognized as an asset to the property.

The first cost of planting shade-trees is very small compared with the other assessments for street improvements. The cost of planting trees properly is a very small percentage of the cost of the improvement of the roadway proper. While the use of the road will cause it to deteriorate and it will need repairs, the trees, when properly cared for, will thrive and grow. Their first cost of setting out will be insignificant when compared with their increased value a number of years after planting.

Finally, the uplifting influence of an environment of trees is such as to make people not only happier but better. A modern progressive city possesses three assets—its industries, its commerce, and its appearance, the outward and visible evidence of character. "Show me your town or city and I will tell you the kind and quality of your citizens," is a rule of universal application invariably correct. The *morale* of a people is unquestionably in exact keeping with the outward and manifest appearance of the municipal home. Few things contribute more to the cultivation of local pride and civic patriotism than beautiful trees in the parks and in the streets.

CHAPTER II

SELECTION OF TREES FOR STREET USE

As important as the task of planting shade-trees is the problem of selecting the proper species. In tree-planting, perhaps more than in most other work, great care, foresight, and judgment are required. The street of mature trees looks quite different from the street of young saplings; yet it is the selection of young trees, their proper setting apart, and their care after planting that make the beautiful street possible.

In every undertaking there should be a well-defined object toward the attainment of which every effort should be directed. In the planting of shade-trees, as in the construction of a building, the plan for the completed work should be determined in advance. The tree-planter must picture to himself how his work will look a great number of years later; and it rests with him whether the result is to be one of satisfaction or regret.

PICTURE OF IDEAL STREET

What shall the image of the ideal street be? Looking down the long perspective we observe that but one species of tree has been planted throughout its entire length. These trees are alike in size. The distance between them is uniform, and is such that, when the trees mature, their out-stretching limbs will not meet; but will leave sufficient space between the trees for the admission of light and the free circulation of air. Other elements that contribute to the making of the ideal street have not been overlooked. Each tree has a neat and substantial guard that effectively protects it from harm, and these guards contribute their share to the beauty of the street by being all alike. There is also evidence that the trees have been judiciously pruned, for no low and drooping branches obstruct the vista of the street.

Good judgment has been exercised in the selection of the tree for this model street. The system of branching is pleasing, and there is symmetry in its general outline; the head is well filled, being neither too open nor too compact; there is the necessary strength in the branches to sustain their own weight, and the leaves remain in a healthy condition till they are ready to fall in the autumn. The perspective of a street, as shown in the frontispiece, is strikingly beautiful at all seasons of the year, when the trees are bare of foliage or when they are in blossom or in leaf.

QUALITIES THAT STREET-TREES SHOULD POSSESS

From a natural standpoint every tree is interesting: the outline, the mode of branching, the bark, the leaf, the flower, and the fruit are all worth studying. Considered from the standpoint of adaptability for street-planting, a tree must possess certain characteristics to be desirable.

Hardiness.—In the first place it must be hardy and capable of withstanding the unfavorable conditions of city life; such as those of poor soil, heat, drought, smoke, and dust. Street-trees are usually unprotected from heavy storms, and they should have strength to resist winds, sleet, and snow. They should possess the ability to endure transplanting well, and be easily propagated.

Straightness and Symmetry.—A tree planted on a lawn may have the branches drooping, the stem crooked, and the shape unsymmetrical; but in this case these oddities in its habits are in themselves elements of beauty. A tree, in order to be adapted for street use, however, must have a straight stem, a rounded, well-filled head and be symmetrical in growth. Its shape is to be, in a certain sense, formal; but, at the same time, it should not be produced entirely by artificial pruning. The tree must lend itself to the requirements of the public use of the highway and preserve, as far as possible, its natural habit of growth.

Immunity from Insect Attack.—In the selection of shade-trees, their relative immunity from insect attack is a point to be considered. While there are few trees that are absolutely free from pests, some trees enjoy greater immunity than others, and, if otherwise desirable, such trees should be preferred.

Abundance of Shade.—Trees that retain their foliage in good condition throughout the summer and show changes of color in autumn are most desirable. Trees that naturally grow an open, scraggly head are not adequate for shade production, and, again, a dense shade during the summer is objectionable because it cuts off sunlight, prevents the growth of grass under the trees, and retards the drying of the highway after rain.

Cleanliness.—Cleanliness in habits of growth is an essential characteristic of good street-trees. The falling of leaves, twigs, bark, flowers, and fruits keep the sidewalks in a state of untidiness, while slippery fruits are dangerous as well as unsightly. Tempting flowers or fruits cause people to injure the trees, and it is manifestly out of place to attempt to grow trees for their fruit on the street.

Longevity. — The ideal street-tree must also be of medium growth and long-lived. The desirability of having good-sized shade-trees, as soon as possible after planting, is admitted; but it is unfortunate that the trees growing most rapidly are not the most desirable. They are short-lived, the wood is soft and easily broken by the wind, and money spent on them is worse than wasted.

FEW SPECIES ANSWER REQUIREMENTS

Although we have more than five hundred native species of trees, they do not all possess the same kinds of usefulness. Many of them are valuable for their timber, others are cultivated for their fruit, and a great number are desirable for parks and lawns. That comparatively few are adapted for street use will not be a surprising fact if some of the qualities that shade-trees must possess are recalled. Only a limited number of trees are sufficiently hard to withstand city conditions, easy to transplant, straight and symmetrical in growth, immune from insect attack, free from the litter of flowers and fruit, and long-lived.

CHAPTER III

SPECIES FOR STREET-PLANTING

I⊤ is appreciated by the writer that any attempt made to give a list of trees suitable for street-planting must necessarily be inadequate. The choice of material is one phase of tree-planting which cannot be of general application to cities situated in different sections of the country. A planter can usually receive valuable help from his State Experiment Station. Frequently, however, the same species will not do as well in one part of a city as in another, or even in different parts of the same street. Only very careful study of local conditions and experience, extending over a period of years, can aid in determining what species to plant. One of the best ways perhaps of deciding upon this point is to note the trees in one's vicinity and see which do best.

Study and experimentation reveal the fact that the number of trees suitable for street-planting in any locality is very limited. This need not be surprising if the severe conditions under which city trees grow are recalled. In the city of Washington, where the street-trees have been under municipal control since 1872, some thirty varieties of trees have been experimented with. Now all of the desirable street-trees of that city can be included in ten or twelve varieties. The same is true of the city of Paris, where the list of species, represented by more than a hundred individ-

PLATE 1.—THE MAPLES.

1. Sycamore Maple, leaves and fruit.   2. Ash-Leaved Maple, leaves and fruit.
3-6. Norway Maple: 3. Winter twig.   4. Leaves and fruit.   5. Flowers.
6. Street of Norway Maples: North Eighteenth Street, East Orange, N. J.
Four years after planting.

uals, numbers eleven. The species represented by more than a thousand specimens number nine.

It has been thought best, however, to give a list of the trees from which selections for street-planting are generally made, in the hope that this list will be helpful to the planter in selecting his material under certain conditions. The trees are described from the point of view of their desirability or undesirability for street-planting. Undoubtedly there are trees other than those enumerated which, under favorable conditions of soil, climate, and care, will make good street-trees.

THE MAPLES

Norway Maple (*Acer platanoides* Linn.).—This tree appears to be the best maple that we have for street use. It comes to us from Europe, its range extending from Norway to Switzerland. It withstands city conditions well and seems to have remarkable resistance to insect attack. While the tussock moth and the leopard moth frequently injure the tree, the greatest damage is sometimes done by certain species of plant lice which lodge themselves on the under side of the leaves, causing them to dry, curl up, and fall from the tree. The natural enemies of the plant lice, however, are very numerous, and the spraying of this species of tree is seldom necessary.

On streets where the houses are in solid rows this species of tree is to be preferred, for the reason that it does not grow so large as the native hard maple. The trees should be set about thirty-eight feet apart. Care must be taken to prevent their heading too low and making too dense a shade. This can be easily done by timely and skilful pruning.

PLATE 2.—SUGAR MAPLE.

1. Flowers.   2. Leaves and fruit.   3. Winter twig.   4. Tree in winter.

PLATE 3.—STREET OF SUGAR MAPLES.

Midland Avenue, East Orange, N. J.   Thirty-five years old.   View taken after the trees were pruned to a uniform height.

The Norway maple bursts into a profuse bloom in the latter part of April and early May, and is densely covered with greenish-yellow flowers. They come out of the same buds as the leaves, but develop much more rapidly, the leaves being only half grown when the flowers begin to turn to seed. In the same cluster may be found separate pistillate and staminate flowers, and some flowers having both pistils and stamens. The pistillate flowers mature into samaras, or keys, with widely divergent wings. The fruit does not become ripe until the fall, although it is fully grown in late spring. The leaves have a marked resemblance to those of the sugar maple, but they are darker and generally a little larger. The leaf-stem exudes an acrid milky sap, which quickly coagulates. This peculiarity of the tree makes it easily recognized. It has closely fissured bark, and grows a round, compact head. The winter buds are much larger than those of the sugar maple.

The Norway maple is very hardy and easily transplanted. It is always rich in appearance, and looks attractive on a street when other trees begin to show the waning of summer. It puts forth its leaves earlier in the spring and retains its verdure later in the season than our native maples. Its leaves turn a clear yellow before falling.

Sycamore Maple (*Acer pseudo-platanus* Linn.).—This is also a European tree, and it takes its name from the fact that its leaves bear a resemblance to the sycamore. In its habit of growth it follows the Norway maple, excepting that the top is not so compact. It is not so hardy as the Norway maple, however, nor is there anything distinctive about the tree to make it preferable to the other hard maples. It is also greatly subjected to the attacks of borers, and is not so desirable for street use.

Sugar Maple (*Acer saccharum* Marsh.).—Hardy, erect, of symmetrical habit and with a well-filled, rounded head, the sugar maple is an ornament on any street. In the forest it frequently rises to sixty or seventy feet without a branch. When growing in the open or on a street it sends out stout, upright branches ten or twelve feet from the ground, forming, while the tree is young, a narrow, egg-shaped head, which ultimately spreads into a broad, round-topped dome. When set on a street the trees should be from forty to forty-five feet apart, to allow for free development in growth and non-interference when near maturity.

The flowers of the sugar maple, which come out in early May, are greenish-yellow and rather inconspicuous. The staminate and the pistillate flowers are borne either on different trees or on different flower stalks of the same cluster on the same tree. The staminate flowers drop off in the latter part of May, but the pistillate flowers mature into the winged fruit called a samara, or key.

Most of the splendor of our trees in the woods and on the streets in the early autumn is due to the brilliant coloring of the sugar maple. It glows in yellow, orange, and red. The beauty of the sugar maple in the summer and in the fall is not lost after the falling of the leaves. During the winter the erect, shapely, and symmetrical outline of the tree is clearly brought out. The buds are narrow and sharp-pointed, and the twigs and branches form a fine network against the sky. The limbs of the trees are smooth and clean. In the old trees the bark of the trunk breaks away by long, shallow fissures, with curling ridges, giving the trunk a plowed appearance. When properly pruned, the trees make a low archway, giving the street a very pleasing perspective.

PLATE 4.—RED MAPLE.

1. Leaves and fruit.   2. Staminate and pistillate flowers.   3. Winter twig.
4. Tree in winter.   5. Leaves.

While naturally the sugar maple is very beautiful, it unfortunately does not thrive in cities. Its requirements as to soil and water are extremely exacting, and its foliage is very sensitive to dust and smoke, especially during periods of drought. The sugar maple borer and the leopard moth are the chief enemies of the sugar maple, and the death of limbs and of entire trees is frequently due to the work of these pests. Another pest that does considerable injury to this tree is the woolly maple scale. The natural range of the sugar maple is from Newfoundland to Georgia, and westward to Manitoba and Texas.

Red Maple (*Acer rubrum* Linn.).—Although it is sometimes called a soft maple, the red maple makes a very good street-tree. Its wood is softer than that of the sugar or the Norway maple, and the tree grows a little faster than either of these, but its frame is admirably adapted to resist heavy winds. Its branches are short, numerous, and erect, but not heavy or spreading enough to be torn loose from the trunk like those of the silver maple. It naturally grows a low, compact, rounded head, and, as it seldom attains its full size when planted in cities, it is well adapted to narrow streets.

The red maple was appropriately named. Its tiny red blossoms are among the earliest to appear in the latter part of March and early April. Especially bright in color are the trees bearing the pistillate, or female flowers; the staminate, or male flowers, are of a lighter hue. The pistillate flowers ripen into scarlet keys or samaras in early May. All summer long the light green leaves swing on red stems, and in the early autumn the tree stands preeminent in the beauty of its scarlet foliage. The red maple looks well at all ages and at all seasons. While young, its smooth, gray bark affords a pleasing contrast to its bright green foliage, and in the winter the fineness of its branches and the slightly upward turn of the slender twigs impart to it a grace possessed by few other native trees.

The tree is generally distributed throughout eastern North America and naturally grows in low swamp lands, and loves the borders of streams, which it sometimes covers to the exclusion of other trees. Hence it requires a moderately rich and rather moist soil when planted on a street.

The tree grows rather slowly when first transplanted, and is apt to look less promising than the hard maples; but when it is once established it makes rapid progress. The red maple is moderately free from insect attack. Sometimes it is a prey of the leopard moth, and frequently in the early summer these trees are infested with plant lice that cause the leaves to curl. The plant lice, however, seldom do much damage, but the leopard moth requires the same treatment as in the case of the hard maple. The trees should be planted about thirty-eight or forty feet apart when set on the streets.

Box Elder or **Ash-Leaved Maple** (*Acer negundo* Linn.).— The box elder has a wide natural range. Its habitation extends from the eastern slope of the Alleghany Mountains west to the foothills of the Rockies, and south to Texas. The tree is of rapid growth and is very extensively used in cities in the middle part of the United States. It is not native along the Atlantic coast, but is planted for ornament and shade.

White or **Silver Maple** (*Acer saccharinum* Linn.).—While the sugar maple, the Norway maple, and the red maple make admirable street-trees, the white maple is one of the poorest. The characteristic that has recommended it for most

PLATE 5.—WHITE MAPLE.

1. Winter twigs: A, Flower buds; B, Leaf buds.   2. Leaves and fruit.   3. Staminate and pistillate flowers.   4. Row of White Maples, about twenty years old, almost entirely destroyed by insects and wind-storms.   The White Maple makes a poor street-tree.

lanting in the past is the rapidity of its growth;
growth implies, as a rule, short life and brittle,
l. It is so with the white maple. Its wood is not
d its mode of branching is such that when its
ome large they cannot sustain their own weight.
ommon thing after a storm to find a great many
mbs of the white maple.
e the other trees of the same group, this tree does
a compact head of fine branches, but usually
ten or twelve feet above the ground into three or
four secondary stems, forming a wide, spreading head with
drooping branches. The twigs hang down from the tree
something like those of the weeping willow, and it is this
habit that makes it very difficult to prune the tree and keep
the branches a certain height above the ground. The tree
suggests the elm in outline, except that its limbs do not possess the graceful arching of the elm, but shoot obliquely upward in almost straight lines. Its rapidity of growth makes
it sometimes too large for ordinary city streets, so that old
trees are often cut back to a few main stubs above the
trunk. A new top is soon formed by suckers that rise from
the shortened limbs, but the tree's symmetry is lost forever.

The white maple is one of the first trees to blossom in the
early spring. Its tiny flowers open during the first warm
days of the late winter or early spring, long before the
appearance of its leaves and a week or two before the blos-
soming of the red maple or the elm. The staminate and
pistillate flowers are borne on different trees. The fruit of
the white maple ripens in April and May, about the time
when the leaves unfold. The samaras, or keys, are larger
than those of the other maples.

The fruit of the maples usually ripens in the autumn and

germinates the following spring. The seeds of the red and the white maples, however, ripen at the end of a few weeks after the trees flower, fall to the ground and germinate at once. The leaves of the silver maple are deeply divided, and are a bright pale green above and silvery white beneath. In a light breeze the under sides of the leaves are exposed, giving the entire tree a silvery appearance.

The white maple can be readily recognized by its light brown bark, which, from the old trunks, peels off in long pieces, free at either end and attached to the middle. The wood is soft and perishable. The breaking of the limbs in storms causes the rough ends that remain to dry, and these decay and carry disease to the heart of the main limbs. In a short time the entire tree suffers and looks unsightly.

Numerous insect pests prey upon this species, among which are the cottony maple scale, the tussock moth, the bag worm, the leopard moth and other borers. The tree requires the greatest care. It gives much trouble by the breaking of its limbs, and in the end it does not make a beautiful shade-tree. Many persons a generation ago made the mistake of planting a great number of these trees on the streets. The rapidity of growth was the only point considered, and now, while the hard maples set out at the same time are healthy and thriving, the white ones are in a condition of decay. When selecting a tree for street-planting the white maple should be avoided.

THE POPLARS

Carolina Poplar (*Populus deltoides* Marsh.).—Planted within recent years more extensively than the white maple, and possessing even greater disadvantages as a shade-tree, is the Carolina poplar, or cottonwood. As in the case of the

PLATE 6.—CAROLINA POPLAR.

1. Winter twig.   2. Mesh of roots removed from 4-inch tile sewer.   3 and 4. Carolina Poplars and Norway Maples, thirteen years after planting.   5. Leaves of
Carolina Poplar.

PLATE 7.—CAROLINA AND LOMBARDY POPLARS.

1 and 2. Carolina Poplars disfigured by severe pruning. 3. Staminate flowers of Carolina Poplar. 4. Street of Lombardy Poplars: Ninth Street, S. E., corner G Street, Washington, D. C. Fifteen years old.

white maple, its rapidity of growth is the only point considered by many persons and all its bad habits are lost sight of.

One of the incongruities connected with the Carolina poplar, that appear to any one who has studied this tree at all, is the fact that its rapidity of growth, which is the characteristic often sought, is something that the planter tries to counteract soon after the tree is set out. In other words the man who plants a poplar knows—or if he does not, the nursery man will tell him—that the tree must be headed back frequently to cause it to spread. The result is that every year the limbs are cut back and the top is reduced to a few stubs.

In the meantime the trunk continues its growth, and after a few years of such treatment the result is a tree of abnormal shape—one that has a thick trunk and small top. So far the tree has required constant attention, but it has not given much shade nor has it been an object of beauty. On the other hand, if a hard maple or other tree of like habit and growth had been planted in its place it would have produced naturally what, with the poplar, was attempted artificially—namely, a medium-sized tree with a rounded, compact head.

If it is allowed to grow untouched the Carolina poplar in a short time becomes too large for the average street. It does not produce an oval head, but shoots upward to a great height. The illustrations, Plate 6, Figs. 3 and 4, show the comparative rates of growth of the Carolina poplar and the Norway maple. In these cases, the trees were set out at the same time, thirteen years ago, on opposite sides of the same street. The Norway maples are now eight inches in diameter, of medium height and of round-shaped head; whereas, the Carolina poplars are twenty-one inches in diameter and have grown so high as to completely hide the house from view. The beauty of the Norway maples will increase with age and add to the attractiveness of the house; but in a few years the poplars will have reached maturity and have begun to decay.

The wood of this species is very weak and extremely brittle. In storms a great many limbs break and not only disfigure the tree, but become a source of danger. The tree sends out many roots near the surface of the ground, that in time become so thick that they raise the flagstones and crack concrete walks. The trunks also become so thick at the base that they push the curbstones out of line. The poplar belongs to the willow family, and, like the other members of the group, loves water. If there is the slightest crevice in a sewer-pipe in the vicinity of a tree its fine rootlets will penetrate the pipe and form a compact mesh of fibers. In a short time this stops the flow of water. Plate 6, Fig. 2, shows such a network of rootlets taken out of a four-inch sewer-pipe.

When in flower, fruit, or leaf, the Carolina poplar is an undesirable object on a street. The flowers appear in March and April before the leaves and, like those of the willow, the staminate and the pistillate flowers are borne on different trees. The staminate trees are densely covered with aments four or five inches long, which ripen in a short time, drop to the ground, and lie in heaps that make the sidewalks slippery. The trees bearing pistillate flowers mature their fruit in May. This consists of aments of small capsules which, on maturing, split open and shed a white, cottony mass of seeds. These fill the meshes of doors and window-screens, and stick to the clothing of passers-by. Pistillate trees when planted become an exasperation to the whole neighborhood. In June, when other trees are at their best, the leaves of this tree begin to drop and keep the street littered all summer until the final shedding of the leaves in the fall.

With so many bad habits and no redeeming traits, it is little wonder that in many towns it is forbidden to plant poplars and in others orders have been issued for their removal. In Albany an ordinance was passed in 1871 which provides that no person in that city shall plant or maintain a cottonwood, and any person who allows such tree to remain on his street premises is guilty of a misdemeanor, punishable by a fine of ten dollars. Pursuant to this law, which is still in force, all the cottonwoods in the streets of Albany were cut down.

The "poplar habit" is a short-sighted one and an expensive one in the long run. Every part of the tree of this species possesses some undesirable feature: the rootlets, the roots, the trunk, the branches, the flower, the leaf, and the fruit; and for these reasons it is felt that there is no other tree on our streets that is so objectionable as the Carolina poplar. If other trees will grow, the Carolina poplar should not be planted, or, if used at all, it should be planted with the plan of cutting the trees out within a few years.

Lombardy Poplar (*Populus italica* Mœnch).—For very narrow streets and sidewalks, the spire-shaped, erect form of the Lombardy poplar is sometimes available. The Lombardy poplar is picturesque, a single tree properly placed being sometimes very effective. The tree is called the "exclamation point" in landscape architecture. It is very tall and has little spread. Its branches, of almost equal length at the base and at the top of the tree, point upward at a sharp angle with the trunk. When planted close together these trees make an admirable windbreak.   On the street they give little shade.   While the tree grows very rapidly, it is short-lived, and hence it is only in extremely special cases that its use as a street-tree is advisable.

THE OAKS

While on the one hand there seems to be a general desire to plant rapidly growing trees, such as the soft maple and the Carolina poplar, there is, on the other, a popular notion that the oaks are "slow growers," and for that reason officials sometimes meet with opposition when they attempt to plant these trees.   On closer study, however, it will be found that the oaks recommended for street-planting grow as rapidly as the hard maples and are some of the best shade-trees for cities.   They are strong, durable, and beautiful, and have practically no insect enemies.   Some of the finest streets of Eastern cities are planted with oaks. Some of the streets of Flushing, Long Island, admirably illustrate what municipal authorities try to accomplish, namely the uniform planting of one species of tree on a street.   There are many examples in that city of thoroughfares set with elms and maples, but the finest in appearance are the streets of pin oaks.   Of all species planted in the city of Washington, the oaks make the finest appearance and produce the most striking effect on a street.   There are in all about five miles of streets planted with pin oaks in that city, the finest stretch being half a mile long on East Pennsylvania Avenue, between Eleventh Street and the eastern branch of the Potomac.

Rapidity of growth is not the most desirable characteristic of a shade-tree.   Besides, the terms rapid growth and slow growth are only relative.   On comparison it will be

PLATE 8.—THE OAKS.

1. Red Oak, leaves and fruit.   2. Pin Oak, leaves and fruit.   3. White Oak,
leaves and fruit.   4. Red Oak, flowering twig: A, Pistillate flowers;
B, Staminate flowers; C, Partly grown acorns of preceding year.   5. Street
of Pin Oaks: Pennsylvania Avenue, S. E., at Thirteenth Street, Washington, D. C.   Nineteen years old.

found that there is little difference in the rate of growth of the good shade-trees.

In a pamphlet on "Tree-Planting on Streets and High-ways," by the late William F. Fox, Superintendent of the New York State Forests, is given a table of the growth-rate of some well-known species of trees. Beginning with a three-inch sapling, the trees here named will in twenty years, under favorable conditions, attain a diameter approx-imately as follows:

	Inches		Inches
White or Silver Maple	21	Yellow Locust	14
American Elm	19	Hard Maple	13
Sycamore or Buttonball	18	Horse-chestnut	13
Tulip-tree	18	Honey Locust	13
Basswood	17	Red Oak	13
Catalpa	16	Pin Oak	13
Red Maple	16	Scarlet Oak	13
Ailantus	16	White Ash	12
Cucumber-tree	15	White Oak	11
Chestnut	14	Hackberry	10

It will be seen from this that there is no difference in growth between the hard maple and the red, the pin and the scarlet oaks. The oaks make little headway during the first and second years after transplanting, but after that time their growth is very rapid, in many cases exceeding that of the hard maples.

Perhaps one of the reasons for the existing prejudice against the oak is that it has not received as fair a test as other trees. In Chapter V, the importance of developing the root system of a tree by frequent transplanting in the nursery is dwelt upon. It is only during the last ten or fif-teen years, since the demand for oaks has grown, that nurs-eries have begun to cultivate these trees on a large scale.

As a result the nursery-trained oaks grow as fast as the hard maples.

Pin Oak (*Quercus palustris* Linn.).—Planted more extensively than others of the genus is the pin oak. Its characteristic pyramidal form distinguishes it from most deciduous trees. The stem rises like an unbroken shaft. The branches are slender and stretch out almost horizontally, those at the bottom being the longest. Its deeply cut, light green, shining leaves give the foliage a massing that is fernlike in grace. The lower branches have a tendency to droop; but this habit can be corrected by proper pruning. The dense branching of this tree causes some of the twigs to die, and it is these spurlike projections from the branches that form the "pins" which give the tree its common name.

The oaks have two sets of flowers—staminate, or male and pistillate, or female. The two sets of flowers are borne on the same tree, and hence the flowers are said to be monœcious—of one household.

Some oaks, such as the white oak, mature their acorns the same season in which they flower; but the pin oak belongs to the group of biennials—the oaks that take two years for the fruit to mature. In autumn, after the spring flowering, the acorns of these trees are only partly grown; they remain in that condition during the winter, continue their growth the next summer, and mature in the fall of the following year.

The leaves of the pin oak turn a deep scarlet in autumn, and as in the case of most of the oaks, they fall late in the season. They are not like the leaves of the white oak, however, some of which remain on the trees all winter.

Red Oak (*Quercus rubra* Linn.).—There is a street in the city of Washington which once seen cannot be forgotten. It is Twelfth Street, between North and South B Streets, and is planted with red oaks, the gorgeous beauty of which cannot fail to impress itself on the mind of every observer. See Plate 9.

All prejudices against the oak as a shade-tree must disappear on beholding that street. The red oak grows faster than any other native oak, and in a greater variety of soils. It forms a round or oval shaped head, and its large, dark green leathery leaves give it a richness possessed by few other trees. There is no American tree more prized in Europe than the red oak, which has been cultivated there for two centuries. It is the brilliant foliage of the red oak which is conspicuous in the English parks in the autumn, when the native species of that country fall without the bright coloring which we always expect in our autumn woods.

In May the red oak is fairly draped with the long yellow catkins, forming the staminate flowers. The pistillate flowers are extremely tiny, and these, after being fertilized, mature into acorns the following year.

Scarlet Oak (*Quercus coccinea* Muench.).—While the pin oak and the red oak are the trees most extensively planted as shade-trees, the scarlet oak is coming to be recognized as superior to both, while in hardiness and rapidity of growth it is equal to either. When growing in the open the scarlet oak forms a round, domelike head. The leaves are a bright shiny green, borne on slender petioles that cause them to respond to every breeze. The splendor of our autumnal forests owes much to the color of the scarlet oaks. The tints of other oaks are beautiful, but they are pale before the gleam of the scarlet.

White Oak (*Quercus alba* Linn.).—The white oak is the

PLATE 9.—STREET OF RED OAKS.

Twelfth Street, West, between North and South B Streets, Washington, D. C.   Twenty years old.

noblest tree of its race, and is justly called the king of the forest. It is superior in vigor and longevity, and attains a greater spread than the other oaks. As a street-tree, however, it has fewer points to recommend it than the other members of the group that have been treated. It grows much more slowly than either the pin, the red, or the scarlet oak. Its red and russet colored autumn leaves are very persistent, often clinging to the tree the entire winter. This is a feature which may be regarded with unfailing interest in the forest, but in the city it makes the trees rather objectionable because of the continued litter of the street.

The white oak belongs to the group of oaks that mature their acorns in one season. Other things being equal the oaks require more care in transplanting than the maples. The wood is harder and the roots dry more rapidly. The first year after these trees are planted, their growth is very slow. During the second and third years, however, the trees make a remarkable growth and an increase of a foot or more in height may be expected yearly. When the oaks are set out the twigs must be cut back almost to the main stem. By this means the draft on the roots is reduced, it gives the tree a chance to reestablish itself, and the top makes up the original loss in a very short time. See Fig. 13.

Other oaks that are sometimes planted on streets and highways in the Northern States are swamp white oak (*Quercus bicolor* Willd.) and chestnut oak (*Quercus prinus* Linn.).

THE LINDENS

American Linden (*Tilia americana* Linn.).—This tree, which is also known as basswood, commends itself as a shade-tree in many ways. It is a vigorous grower. When young it is of pyramidal form and eventually becomes a large, round-headed tree. Its foliage is of light green color, very large and abundant, and produces a dense shade. The leaves are heart-shaped and always one sided. They open late in the spring, and in the latter part of June are followed by clusters of fragrant flowers. They are yellowish-white and are suspended from curious ribbonlike appendages called bracts.

The flowers mature into pealike seeds which drop from the tree in the fall of the year. The bracts to which the seed clusters are attached act as parachutes, which launch the fruit some distance beyond the tree. The bark of the linden is rather smooth, with shallow, close furrows. The main trunk of this tree frequently extends upward undivided to the top, with small branches growing from the limbs all the way up. This characteristic of the linden is especially marked in young trees. Large ones generally have two or three main trunks, like the elm or white maple. After the leaves have fallen the linden displays a graceful outline, making it attractive in winter.

The American linden is at its best before midsummer. After that time the tree grows coarse and the leaves begin to show the effects of the attacks of the numerous insects to which it is a prey. It is the susceptibility to insect attack that forms the objectionable feature of the tree. In early summer plant lice cover the leaves with patches of honey dew, and the sticky surfaces catch dust and smoke. The leaves are also subject to the attack of a fungus which gives them the appearance of being covered with soot. American lindens are sometimes completely defoliated by the caterpillars of the tussock moth, and are seriously injured by borers. As a result of the insect attacks the leaves turn

PLATE 10.—THE LINDENS.

1. American Linden, leaves and fruit. 2. European Linden in winter. 3. European Linden, leaves and flowers. 4. European Linden, winter twig. 5. Street of American Lindens: Massachusetts Avenue, N. E., at Eleventh Street, Washington, D. C. Thirty years old.

and fall prematurely. Their faded yellow is not like the gold of the beech and hickory leaves.

While the American linden possesses natural characteristics desirable for a shade-tree, these are largely offset by its numerous insect enemies. The tree also requires a deep rich soil, is less tolerable of city conditions, and requires greater care than other trees.

European Linden (*Tilia europœa* Linn.).—In beauty, symmetry, and grace few trees surpass or equal the European linden. It grows perfectly straight, the trunk and main limbs are subdivided into a great many twigs forming a compact, oval head. When the tree is left to grow naturally, the lower limbs are drooping, but when trimmed up the branches acquire a graceful, upward turn.

The leaves of the European linden are more regularly heart-shaped and smaller than those of the American linden, and the twigs are more slender and numerous. In winter the fine twigs of this species make a delicate network against the sky. The flowers of the European linden are very fragrant, and are borne in clusters attached to a ribbon-like bract very much resembling the American linden. The pealike fruit matures in the fall, but is very persistent, some of the bracts remaining on the trees all winter.

While also subject to the attacks of plant lice and caterpillars, the European linden withstands city conditions a little better than the native tree and preserves the natural beauty of its foliage later in the season. It grows into a medium-sized shapely tree, and is especially adapted for narrow streets.

There are a number of varieties of the American and the European lindens which make good street-trees, of which may be mentioned the following: the silver-leaved linden

(*Tilia argentea*), the Crimean, or yellow-twigged linden (*Tilia dasystyla*), and the large-leaved European linden (*Tilia platyphylla*). *Tilia dasystyla* is one of the best varieties for street-planting. The leaves are leathery and tough, and remain green until a hard frost, then they fall at one time.

THE ELMS

White or **American Elm** (*Ulmus americana* Linn.).— Standing absolutely alone for its especial kind of beauty, the white elm is deservedly the most familiar and popular of our native trees. No other tree combines such strength with so much grace. It is the striking ornament of New England landscapes, and in many towns the white elm is the predominant tree. New Haven has attained national fame as the Elm City.

At all seasons of the year the elm is beautiful. In summer it rises like a great fountain of brilliant green, and in winter the detail of the arching limbs and pendulous branches stands out in relief against the sky. The white elm is one of the first trees to blossom in the spring. As early as the latter part of February, or the early part of March, the flower-buds begin to swell, and shortly afterward the small reddish-brown blossoms appear, so tiny that they frequently pass unnoticed. The fruit of the elm, or samara, as it is called, matures in May, when the leaves unfold.

Flat, oval-shaped wings, about half an inch long, surround the small seeds and help the wind to scatter them from the parent tree. The leaves of the white elm are unequal at the base, are rough above and downy beneath. In autumn they turn a brown or golden yellow.

Considered from the standpoint of adaptability for street-planting, it has been found that in spite of the natural

PLATE 11.—AMERICAN ELM.

1. Winter twig.   2.   Flowers.   3. Fruit and developing leaves.   4. Leaves.
5. Tree in winter.

PLATE 12.—STREET OF WHITE ELMS.

East Capitol Street, near Sixth Street, N. E., Washington, D. C.   Thirty years old.   Distance from building line to building line, 160 feet, width of roadway, 50 feet.

beauty of the white elm, it has a great many limitations. The greatest objection to this tree is its susceptibility to the attacks of more insect pests than any other one species of tree. Some of its enemies are the elm-leaf beetle, the tussock moth, the leopard moth, elm borers, the elm-bark louse, the spiny elm caterpillar, the bag worm, the gipsy moth, and the brown tail moth. Of these, the elm-leaf beetle, the tussock and the leopard moths, are the most destructive. The aspect of the elm-trees infested with the beetle is one of devastation. They look as if they had been swept by fire.

The elm is adapted to wide streets, for it grows to a great size. The characteristics that make it one of the most beautiful of our native trees do not develop until the tree is of considerable age. In the ordinary street, especially in places where the houses are close to the sidewalk, the tree has no room. Standing as an individual, the American elm is very picturesque. Lining a broad avenue, the trees form a perfect Gothic archway like a cathedral nave, the beauty of which is not surpassed by any other species. On the street of ordinary width the elm has no place. In the case of this tree, too, more than most other species of trees, provision must be made for regular and thorough spraying to hold the insect enemies in check.

European Elm (*Ulmus campestris* Linn.).—The European elm is sometimes used as a street-tree. In form it is better suited for such planting, as it grows a smaller and more rounded head. It also retains its foliage later in the season. However, the natural advantages of this tree are more than offset by insect pests. The European elm is greedily attacked by the elm-leaf beetle, the destructiveness of which is greater than in the case of the native species.

Horse-Chestnut (*Æsculus hippocastanum* Linn.).—The spring is the redeeming season of the horse-chestnut. When in bloom the tree is a superb sight, "a pyramid of green supporting a thousand pyramids of white."

The unfolding of its leaves is also extremely interesting and beautiful. By opening one of the buds of the tree with a knife in winter one finds the little leaves and miniature flower clusters carefully packed in the downy wool under the gummy scales. When the warm days of spring come, the resinous bud-scales drop off, and the little fuzzy, light green leaves come out of the buds. The leaflets are close together, like the fingers of a tiny hand, and they hang limp from their stems like moths just emerged from their cocoons. The leaves grow with remarkable rapidity, however, and soon the trees become covered with a dense foliage.

The horse-chestnut is a native of southeastern Europe, and has for centuries been a favorite tree for avenues and parks in Europe. One of the finest plantations of horse-chestnuts in the world is that in Bushey Park, near London. Five rows of the trees stand on either side of the avenue, and when they are in bloom the fact is announced in the newspapers. Then the public go to see the sight. This species is extensively used in Paris. There are over 17,000 horse-chestnut trees in the streets of that city.

The tree was first introduced in the United States in 1746. It belongs to the same genus as our native buckeye, with which it is sometimes confused. If one remembers the difference in the leaves, however, it is easy to distinguish the two trees. The leaves of the buckeye are five-fingered, while those of the horse-chestnut are seven-fingered. The horse-chestnut is the sturdier of the two, and the flowers are more profuse and beautiful than those of the buckeye.

PLATE 13.—HORSE-CHESTNUT.

1. Leaves and flowers.   2. Leaf and fruit.   3. Tree in winter.
4. Winter twig.   5. Tree in flower.

While the horse-chestnut possesses many features of natural and historic interest, it has few points that recommend it for use as a street-tree. In early summer the leaves become discolored, shrivel and fall. In fact, this tree is continually dropping something. The bud-scales and the flowers fall in the spring, the leaves in the summer, and the husks and nuts of the fruit in the autumn. The tree is also subject to the attacks of many insect enemies, the chief of which are the leopard moth and the tussock moth. The tree is at its best when grown in the open; but where maples and oaks can be successfully grown there is little in the horse-chestnut to recommend it for street-planting.

THE PLANE TREES

Oriental Plane (*Platanus orientalis* Linn.).—The oriental plane combines, to a greater degree than any other tree, the characteristics of rapid growth with everything that is desirable in shade-trees. It is perfectly hardy, grows a straight stem, and forms a symmetrical, compact, and round head. It has the advantage of the rapid growth of the white maple and the Carolina poplar, and possesses none of their many defects.

The leaves of the oriental plane are very large, and the tree gives ample shade, but, at the same time, the foliage is not too dense. It is disposed to grow rather large, but it may be pruned without injury at any time and with any degree of severity to make it conform to the width of any street.

All points considered, the oriental plane makes such an admirable street-tree that there is a temptation to plant it to the exclusion of other trees. For the last few years it has been most extensively used in the cities of Washington and

PLATE 14.—THE PLANE TREES.

1. Sycamore, winter twig.   2. Sycamore, developing leaves and flowers, upper pistil-
late and lower staminate.   3. Oriental Plane, leaves and fruit.   4. Oriental
Plane, bark.   5. Street of Oriental Planes: S Street, at North Capitol Street,
Washington, D. C.   Twelve years old.

Philadelphia—in greater numbers, in fact, than any other single species of tree. Of the 86,000 trees in the city of Paris, over 26,000 are oriental planes.

The oriental plane is of the same genus as the Western plane or sycamore, or button-ball (*Platanus occidentalis* Linn.), which also makes a splendid street-tree. It resembles our native species in leaf, fruit, and bark, but it grows more compactly and symmetrically than the Western plane. The most striking feature of both species of trees is that they shed their bark as well as their leaves. All trees shed their bark to some degree, as the outer layers yield to the pressure of the growing stem.

The dropping of the bark is noticeable in the silver maple and the shagbark hickory; and it is especially marked in the planes. The bark of the trunk and larger limbs flakes off in great irregular masses, leaving the surface a mottled greenish-white and gray and brown. The characteristic bark is especially noticeable in winter, although the thickest foliage of summer never quite conceals it.

The male and the female flowers of the planes are borne in heads on separate buds of the same twigs. The pistillate flowers ripen into the familiar globular fruits of the planes which remain suspended from the slender stems almost the entire winter. The oriental plane can be readily distinguished from the sycamore after the leaves have fallen. The fruit of the sycamore is generally borne in solitary heads, and in extremely rare cases two heads are found on a single stem. The oriental plane bears from two to four of these globular fruits on a single stem.

The heads of fruit of the planes are composed of thin seeds, about half an inch long, packed tightly around a central spherical core. Each seed is surrounded by hairs that close around it like the ribs of an umbrella.   When the ripe fruit is released the hairs open up and form a little parachute that keeps the seed suspended in the air for a considerable period of time, and enables the wind to carry it far away from the parent tree.

The oriental plane is not troubled by many insect pests. The tussock moth and the fall web-worm sometimes attack it, but they never cause serious injury.   The sycamore is subject to a fungous disease that attacks the young leaves as they come out of the bud, causing them to turn brown and shrivel up.   The European species is less subject to this disease.

Tulip-Tree (*Liriodendron tulipifera* Linn.).—The tulip-tree is one of the largest and most beautiful of our native trees.   It belongs to the magnolia family and, like all the members of that group, it has large, brilliant flowers. Their color is greenish-yellow, with dashes of red and orange, and their resemblance to a tulip is marked.   They open in May, shortly after the development of the leaves, and are borne on stout stems that keep them erect.

The flowers of the tulip are complete.   The fruit of the tulip is a cone, two or three inches long, composed of thin, narrow scales attached to a common axis.   These scales are each a seed surrounded by a thin wing.   The fruit ripens during October, and, beginning at the top of each cone, one by one the seeds become detached from the central axis, and by the aid of the wind each seed is carried some distance from the tree.

The leaves of the tulip are unique in shape, the "chopped off" ends giving them an individuality of their own.   When fully developed the leaves have a tremulous motion, resembling those cf the poplars, and for that reason

PLATE 15.—TULIP-TREE.

1. Tree in winter.   2. Leaves and flower.   3. Fruit in winter, only a few remaining seeds attached to axis.   4. Winter twig.   5. Street of Tulip-Trees, North Capitol Street, at M Street, Washington, D. C.

the tulip is sometimes called the tulip poplar. It is not to be confounded with poplars, however, as there is no relationship between them, the poplars belonging to the willow family.

As a shade-tree the tulip is very beautiful and symmetrical; but it is adapted for only the widest avenues, as it becomes too large for the average street. It thrives best in places where there is a quantity of rich, deep soil, conditions which do not obtain along the street curb. While the tulip is moderately free from enemies, its leaves are subject to the attack of an insect that forms the tulip-tree spot gall. These galls are brown spots covering the surface of the leaves in midsummer. The leaves turn yellow and drop from the trees throughout the season.

The tulip-tree is one of the most difficult trees to transplant. Like all the magnolias, it has tender, succulent roots that dry on the least exposure. It is one of the trees that it is quite impossible to transplant in the fall; for if its roots do not begin immediate growth after planting the tree dies.

White Ash (*Fraxinus americana* Linn.).—Although so far the ash has not been much used in cities, it possesses many characteristics that recommend it for a shade-tree. It is a rapid grower, perfectly hardy in many sections of the country and has no serious insect enemies. It grows straight and symmetrical, and forms a round top. The foliage is pleasing in appearance, growing in irregular wavy masses, and not compact like the maples or the oaks. In fact, some sunlight always finds its way through the foliage of this tree, even in midsummer.

The white ash has compound leaves about ten inches long. They have from five to nine leaflets—usually seven. The leaves are dark green in summer, and in autumn turn

PLATE 16—WHITE ASH.

1. Winter twig.   2. Pistillate flowers.   3. Staminate flowers.   4. Leaf and fruit.
5. Tree in summer.

brownish purple and yellow. Like most trees with large compound leaves, the ash sheds its spray with the foliage in the fall, leaving the erect rigid twigs that somewhat detract from the beauty of the tree in winter. When stripped of foliage the characteristic open head of the tree is marked. The bark is closely furrowed with irregular ridges and the twigs form a network of crosses against the sky.

The staminate, or male flowers, and the pistillate, or female flowers, are borne on separate trees. They open in May before the leaves and are borne in small, compact clusters. The staminate, or male trees, ordinarily shed their flowers about the time the leaves unfold, when the bursting pollen shells are mature. Sometimes the undeveloped male flower clusters are attacked by tiny mites that cause them to change into berrylike growths, which hang on in dry clusters on the ends of the branches. Frequently these abnormal formations, which resemble the familiar oak-galls, are mistaken for the fruit of the ash.

The pistillate, or female flowers, mature into seeds. The fruit of the white ash comes in crowded, drooping panicles which hang upon the branches until after the leaves have fallen, almost until midwinter. On examination it will be found that each seed of the ash is provided with a thin membranous appendage, or wing, which keeps the seed balanced in the air when it drops from the tree and allows the wind to carry it far from the parent tree.

Hackberry (*Celtis occidentalis* Linn.).—The hackberry is a medium-sized tree, which, in its general appearance, resembles the elm. Its straight trunk does not divide until it has attained considerable height, a peculiarity which is an advantage in a street-tree. It is tolerant of many conditions of soil and climate, prefers rich, moist soil, but can

PLATE 17.—SWEET GUM, HACKBERRY, AND GINGKO.

1. Sweet Gum, leaves and fruit.   2. Hackberry in winter.   3. Gingko, winter twig.   4. Gingko, leaves.   5. Street of Gingkos, leading from grounds of the United States Department of Agriculture, Washington, D. C.   Thirty years old.

live in dry situations as well. It is comparatively free from insect pests and diseases. The hackberry has a peculiar bark, covered with hard, warty excrescences.

Gingko (*Gingko biloba* Linn.) (*Salisburia adiantifolia*).— A new and very promising tree for street use is the gingko, a most remarkable species from China and Japan. It is hardy, and is one of the few trees that is entirely free from enemies of any kind. Its natural shape is pyramidal. The branches have a tendency to hug the central stem, while a few limbs shoot outwardly beyond the general contour of the tree. This mode of branching is not perhaps the most ideal for a shade-tree; but by careful pruning the limbs can be made to spread and the head of the tree may be trained into a more oval form. One of the most beautiful and striking examples of the gingko as a street-tree is an avenue leading to the Department of Agriculture Building in Washington, Plate 17, Fig. 5.

The leaf of the gingko is its most curious feature. There is nothing like it in the foliage of trees in America or Europe. It resembles that of the maiden-hair fern, and hence one of the common names of the gingko is the maiden-hair tree. The leaves are two-lobed and parallel veined; that is, there is no midrib with diverging veins as in our native trees. The veins run nearly parallel with each other from the base to the end of the leaf. The foliage of the gingko turns a clear, golden yellow before it drops from the trees in autumn.

What may appear strange is that the gingko belongs to the pine family. It is not an evergreen, however, and in this respect resembles the larch and the bald cypress. The falling of the leaves is but an outward and visible sign of an inward structural difference, which removes the pines from their other neighbors of the forest. It is the flower of a plant that largely determines its position in botanical classification.

The gingko, although differing from the pines in many other ways, is like them in its mode of flowering. The staminate and the pistillate flowers are borne on different branches of the same tree. The female flowers consist of two naked ovules which receive the pollen. These ripen into the fruit of the gingko, which is a fleshy drupe resembling a small plum. The drupes are ill-scented, and are considered by some as an objection to the tree. Gingkos, however, do not fruit until they are about thirty or forty years old, and the fruiting season does not last very long.

Sweet Gum (*Liquidambar styraciflua* Linn.).—In brilliancy of autumn foliage few trees surpass the liquidambar, or sweet gum. The color of its beautiful star-shaped leaves varies from deep red to yellow, and, in addition, some leaves are dark purple and brown. It grows perfectly straight and forms a symmetrical top. Like the magnolias, however, it has succulent roots, and is somewhat difficult to transplant. Naturally, the sweet gum is usually found in wet, rich soil bordering streams or swamps. The average street is too dry for them. When under favorable conditions the trees once become established they are extremely beautiful and more than offset the extra care that is required in transplanting and the litter caused by their fruit.

THE CATALPAS

Hardy Catalpa (*Catalpa Catalpa* (Linn.) Karst.).—The catalpa is an ornamental tree. It has very large leaves and in June is resplendent with pyramid-shaped clusters of flowers resembling those of the horse-chestnut. It naturally

PLATE 18.—CATALPA, AILANTUS, AND HONEY LOCUST.

1. Hardy Catalpa, leaves and flowers. 2. Hardy Catalpa, fruit. 3. Ailantus, leaf and fruit. 4. Honey Locust, leaves and fruit. 5. Street of Honey Locusts: G Street, corner Twelfth Street, S. E., Washington, D. C.

grows crooked, with a short, thick trunk and long strag-
gling branches, and forms an irregular head. These characteristics are against its employment for street-planting.

Western Catalpa (*Catalpa speciosa* Ward.).—This is a
Western species which is very hardy, of rapid growth, and
has proved a much better tree for street use than the
common or hardy catalpa.

Ailantus (*Ailanthus glandulosa* Desf.).—The ailantus,
also spelled ailanthus, is sometimes used for street-planting,
but outside of the fact that it will thrive in the poorest soil
and amid the most unfavorable conditions of city streets
there is very little to recommend it. When young, the
ailantus is vigorous and shapely, if properly trained, and
its large leaves are green until frost, but most old trees present a very scraggly and unsightly appearance. The tree
possesses little grace in winter after the large compound
leaves fall and the thick, rigid twigs are revealed. At blos-
soming time the odor of the staminate or male flowers is
extremely unpleasant. Where other trees will grow the
ailantus should not be considered.

THE LOCUSTS

The Black Locust (*Robinia pseudacacia* Linn.) and the
Honey Locust (*Gleditsia triacanthos* Linn.) are sometimes
used as shade-trees. The former is successfully cultivated
in Paris, where the top is kept small and spherical, and the
branches thickly clustered. If allowed to grow freely, however, this tree does not form a round, compact head, but is
angular in form. Its branches are extremely brittle, its foliage short-lived, its pods persistent and given to sprouting.

In the city of Washington there are a few streets planted
with the honey locust. They do not look so beautiful as

PLATE 19.—STREET OF LIVE OAKS.

Magazine Street entrance to Audubon Park, New Orleans, La.   Spanish moss on trees.   View taken in February.

those planted with other species. Besides, the honey locust gives practically no shade at all. Its foliage is fine and delicate, and comes out very late in the season. In late summer, the long, twisted pods bearing the seeds of the trees are more conspicuous than the leaves. They remain on the trees almost all winter. The sharp, stout thorns, two or three inches long, which are a characteristic feature of these trees make it almost impossible for a man to prune them. Both the black locust and the honey locust are attacked by borers and caterpillars that cause great injury to them.

SPECIES FOR SOUTHERN STATES

The establishment of a Parking Commission in New Orleans, to have charge of the planting and care of street-trees in that city, will act as an incentive to other Southern cities to establish similar departments. On account of the climate and great variety of native flora no section of the land offers greater opportunities for the embellishment of the home and the street than the Southern States. Many of the species described before are hardy in the South. Among the trees that are native, or can be grown only in the Southern States, may be mentioned the following:

Live Oak (*Quercus virginiana* Mil.).—Some of the most magnificent, stately, and highly esteemed trees for street-planting in the Southern States belong to the oak genus, the grandest and most beautiful of which is the live oak. It is an evergreen occurring naturally near the Atlantic coast, from Virginia to Florida and westward along the Gulf of Mexico to Texas. It is one of the most rapid growing of American oaks. Some grand specimens of the live oak may be found in the Audubon and City Parks in New Orleans, Plate 19.

PLATE 20.—SOME SOUTHERN TREES.

1. Pecan in winter, Spanish moss on tree. 2. Great Laurel Magnolia.
3. Water Oak. 4. Avenue of Palmettos. Views taken in February,
New Orleans, La.

The water oak (*Quercus nigra* Linn.), the willow oak (*Quercus phellos* Linn.), and the laurel oak (*Quercus laurifolia* Michx.) are also commonly planted as shade-trees in the streets and squares of the cities and towns of the Southern States.

Great Laurel Magnolia (*Magnolia grandiflora* Linn.).— This is one of the grandest of the evergreen trees of the South, and is well adapted for street-planting. Its massive evergreen leaves and large white blossoms make it most conspicuous. It succeeds best in a rich soil, and should have plenty of room for spreading.

Pecan (*Hicoria pecan* Britt.).—This tree is hardy as far north as Philadelphia. It is a very handsome tree, the largest of the hickories, and is native of rich moist soils of river valleys from Indiana to Iowa, Missouri, and Kansas, south to Alabama and Texas. It is a fine shade and ornamental tree.

Camphor-Tree (*Cinnamomum camphora* Linn.).—This is a fast-growing, handsome evergreen tree, with bright, shiny leaves, symmetrical in growth and thriving even in poor soil. It is a native of Japan. It grows to medium size, and is suitable for narrow streets.

The Palmetto (*Sabal palmetto* Walt.) and the **Desert Palm** (*Neowashingtonia robusta* (Wend.) Britt.) are very generally planted for shade and ornament in the Southern States. The palmetto grows from eastern North Carolina to Florida. The trunk reaches a maximum height of about sixty feet, which is surmounted by a crown of spreading, fan-like leaves, seven to eight feet broad. The desert palm, or Washington palm, is a striking feature of the Colorado desert. It is found in groves or in isolated clumps in wet alkali soil, rising to a height of from fifty to seventy-five feet.

This elegant palm is much planted for ornament in California and Florida.

THE CONIFERS

The conifers cannot be used on the street as shade-trees. Their branching and mode of growth are such as to make them absolutely impossible to prune. They must be left to grow naturally. When growing close together in the forest, a process of natural pruning goes on, the lateral limbs die out for want of light and air, and the trees shoot upward, producing straight, tall trunks. When growing in the open, on the other hand, the lower branches commence near the ground. Any attempt to remove the lower limbs disfigures the tree, and, therefore, while these trees are useful and highly decorative for lawn and park purposes they cannot be used for the street.

CHAPTER IV

STUDIES PRELIMINARY TO PLANTING

PRELIMINARY to planting, a survey of the street must be made. This consists of an examination of the soil, the noting of the width of the street and the sidewalks, the height of the buildings bordering the street, the direction of the street, and all the local conditions that enter into the determination of the choice of species for the street.

The Soil.—A great deal, if not all of the success in tree-growing, depends upon the nature and the preparation of the soil. An examination of the soil will show whether by its nature, extent, and depth it is favorable or unfavorable to tree-growth. It is very seldom that the soil existing along city streets is good for planting. In grading streets and avenues there is always more or less cutting down and filling up, and in either case the original surface soil is rendered unavailable. It then becomes an absolute necessity to make liberal provision of good soil for the future well-being of the tree.

By excavations or borings four or five feet deep, the kind and depth of the soil and the nature of the subsoil should be determined. In the planting of street-trees, where the conditions are sometimes not alike for two successive trees, it is indispensable to make a survey and keep an exact record of the kind of soil where the trees are to be planted, the nature of the adjoining soil and subsoil, the proximity of sewers, water and gas mains to the proposed line of planting, and all other conditions that could influence vegetation favorably or unfavorably. Such records will be found very valuable not only for the planting, but also for the future care of the trees, particularly their watering, fertilizing, and training, and approximation of their length of life.

Soil suitable for tree-planting must contain the elements essential to vegetation, and must be of ample extent to supply the needs of the growing tree. An average light sandy loam, easily worked, uniform, finely grained and smooth to the touch, is ideal for trees. A heavy clay soil is unfavorable for trees, because it is not permeable to water and air, and when it dries it becomes excessively hard and cracks. A soil that is too sandy does not retain moisture necessary to maintain vegetation. A soil containing on the average about 70 per cent. sand, 20 per cent. clay, and 10 per cent. humus is found to be suitable for most trees. Soil of average fertility contains in a dry state .1 per cent. to .2 per cent., by weight, of nitrogen, .1 per cent. to .2 per cent. phosphoric acid, .1 per cent. to .2 per cent. of potash, and .4 per cent. to .6 per cent. of lime. When a soil fulfilling the above conditions is found along the line of the proposed planting, and the subsoil is pervious to water and permits of good drainage, it will produce conditions for good growth and long life of the trees planted.

When choosing soil to replace poor street soil it is well to observe the conditions making up the ideal soil and obtain it, if possible. It is found that soil stripped from an old pasture land, or other land which has had some cultivation, makes the best earth for trees. When doing considerable planting, it is a good plan to prepare a compost heap the year before by putting soil and manure in alternate layers, and turning the pile two or three times in the season to mix them thoroughly. In no case should fresh manure or patent fertilizers be used with the soil.

Amount of Soil.—The amount and extent of soil necessary for the normal development of the root system of trees is about proportional to the spread of the top. It will be readily understood that when trees are planted along sidewalk strips, from four to six feet wide, that good soil ought to exist along the entire line of the planting to a depth of at least three feet. It is very seldom, however, in actual planting operations that the entire soil along the planting strip is removed. In the city of Washington, holes for trees are dug eight feet long, three or three and a half feet wide, and three feet deep, the contents removed and good soil substituted. This is about the size of holes dug for the trees in the city of Paris. This size of hole and quantity of soil give the trees a good start in life, and insure satisfactory growth for at least five or six years. After that the roots will, in most cases, extend into the ordinary surrounding soil, even if it is not of the best description. If at that time the tree shows signs of restricted growth and early casting of leaves, it will be necessary to supply additional good soil beyond the original excavation when the tree was planted. If the original soil is workable it can be improved by cultivation and fertilization, so as to supply the extending roots.

Plantations on excavated ground are generally less favorably situated than those on filled-in ground. The surrounding soil in the former case is apt to be poorer, less workable, and less pervious to moisture than filled-in ground. In the planting of street-trees it is always best for immediate results and for future economy to supply as large a quantity of soil as is possible, in order to insure the establishment and long life of the trees set out.

Subsoil.—If, on account of the impervious nature of the subsoil, moisture is liable to collect and stagnate near the roots and prevent a circulation of air, the soil will have to be underdrained to insure the success of the plantation.

Preparation of the Soil.—How the soil for the tree is to be prepared depends upon the condition of the original ground, whether it is entirely good, partly good, or entirely bad. If the soil is recognized as good and ample, it will always be best to dig the hole of the regulation size and then replace the original soil. The digging up of the soil will make it more pervious to water and render the plant food more available.

If part of the soil is to be replaced, the hole should be dug the full size, and the bad soil removed. The good soil should then be mixed with the remainder and the hole refilled. When all the soil is bad it will have to be entirely replaced. When the soil is entirely or partly replaced, care must be taken to supply enough to allow for settling, which is about $1\frac{1}{2}$ inches to the foot.

The preparation of the hole should precede the planting some months, to allow for the settling of the soil. For spring planting it is best to prepare the holes in the fall, so as to leave more time for the setting of the trees during the spring rush.

ARRANGEMENT OF TREES ON STREET

Parking Strips.—On the street of average width, shade-trees are usually planted on the sidewalk between the curb and the walk. There should be a continuous parking strip provided, at least four feet in width, along which trees may be planted. If the width of the street permits, these strips may be made up to ten feet or more, but a width of four feet is about the minimum space along which trees can be planted. Frequently no planting-strip is provided at all, or it is made so narrow that it is impossible to set out trees.

Width of Roadway.—The determining factor of the width of the roadway is the amount of vehicular traffic it carries, and it should not be made wider than necessary. In the first place it costs more to construct and maintain a wide road than a narrow one. The wider the road the greater the volume of dust, and the closer the road comes to the sidewalk the nearer the dust is to the pedestrians. A broad strip of turf between walk and curb enhances the beauty of the street, and gives the trees a better chance for life and vigor.

In some cities and towns the streets are laid out with no provision for trees, and the widths of the roadway and the sidewalks are not in proportion to the use of the highway. In Carlisle, Pa., for example, most of the streets are sixty feet wide. Although the street traffic is not extensive, the roadways are made forty feet wide and the sidewalks ten feet wide. The houses are built close to the sidewalks, and as soon as the trees become of considerable size the branches grow against the buildings. As a result of such conditions, an ordinance was enacted in Carlisle requiring the setting of the trees in the gutter. It is evident that such a system of tree-planting is very bad. Trees planted in the gutter become an obstruction to the highway, they prevent the running off of storm-water, and prevent the keeping of the roadways clean. Plate 32, Fig. 5.

Divisions of the Street.—The division of the street into walks and drives, and the determination of the number of rows of trees to be set out, will be governed by its width, height of the buildings along the street, and their proximity to the planting-line. On the average street the width from

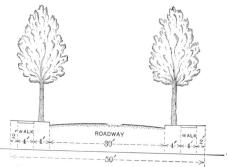

FIG. 1.—Layout of a street fifty feet wide from property line to property line.

fence-line to fence-line is divided into two-fifths for side-walks and three-fifths for the roadway. Residence streets are usually fifty feet wide. This arrangement leaves the sidewalk space ten feet wide, and it can be divided into a 4-foot planting-strip, 4-foot walk, and a 2-foot sod space between the walk and the property-line, as shown in Fig. 1.

Streets sixty feet wide from fence-line to fence-line are

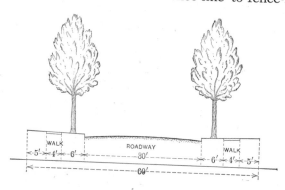

FIG. 2.—Layout of a street sixty feet wide.

of ideal width for residential cities. This width can be
divided into a roadway thirty feet wide and sidewalks fifteen feet wide. A 6-foot planting-strip can be provided on

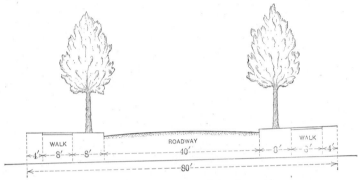

FIG. 3.—Layout of a street eighty feet wide.

a sidewalk of such width, as shown in Fig. 2. A residence
street eighty feet wide may have a roadway forty feet in
width and sidewalks twenty feet wide. The sidewalk may
be divided into an 8-foot lawn-strip, an 8-foot sidewalk,
and a 4-foot strip between the walk and the fence-line, as
shown in Fig. 3. A residence street one hundred feet wide

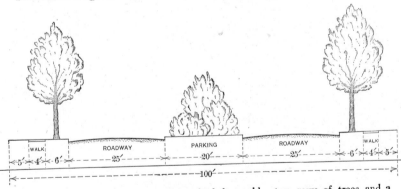

FIG. 4.—Layout of a street one hundred feet wide: two rows of trees and a
parking space for shrubs in centre.

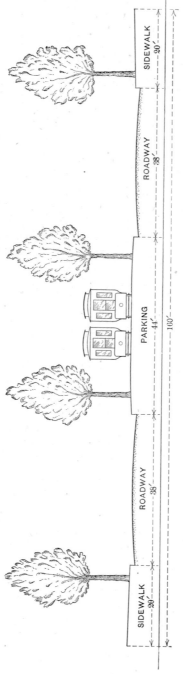

SIDEWALK
20′

ROADWAY
38′

PARKING
44′

ROADWAY
38′

SIDEWALK
20′

100′

Fig. 5.—Layout of Pennsylvania Avenue, Washington, D. C.

may have two roadways separated by a planting-space along its centre. The arrangement is shown in Fig. 4. The central space may be used for shrubs and dwarf trees, but such a street is hardly of sufficient width to permit the planting of more than two rows of large trees, one row along each sidewalk. Avenues or boulevards one hundred and twenty or one hundred and fifty feet wide permit of an arrangement of four rows of trees: two rows along the

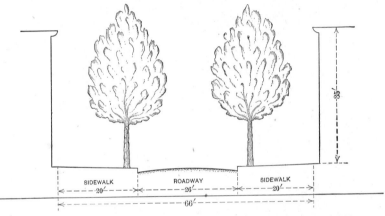

SIDEWALK   ROADWAY   SIDEWALK
20′   26′   20′
66′

FIG. 6.—Streets having buildings thirty-five feet high, on both sides, should have a width of sixty-six feet. The divisions of the street and the positions of the trees are shown.

sidewalks and two rows in the central space. In the city of Washington the streets having four rows of trees are about one hundred and fifty feet in width. Pennsylvania Avenue may be taken as a typical example, shown in Fig. 5.

Height of Buildings.—On residential streets the houses are set back some distance from the sidewalk, twenty feet or more. When this is the case there is more room for the trees to develop. When tall buildings are close to the side-walk, the conditions for growth are not so favorable. In

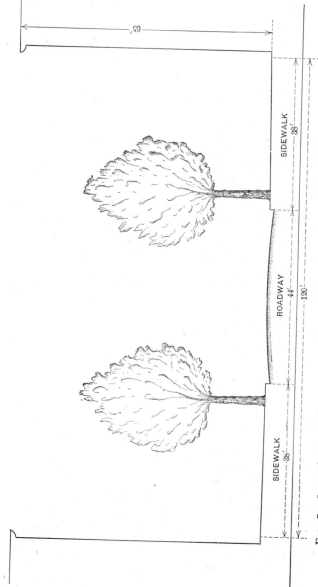

FIG. 7.—Streets having buildings sixty-five feet high should have a width of one hundred and twenty feet. The divisions of the street and the positions of the trees are shown.

Paris the height of buildings is limited to sixty-six feet on streets thirty-three feet wide. On streets less than twenty-six feet wide, the height of buildings is limited to forty feet. In order that street-trees might get enough light to develop vigorously, it is found on the average that streets bounded on both sides with buildings thirty-five feet high should have a width of sixty-six feet, and streets having lines of buildings sixty-five feet high should have a width of one hundred and twenty feet, as shown in Figs. 6 and 7.

On narrow streets having tall buildings, it is possible to maintain trees in good condition by planting a single row in the centre of the roadway, as shown in Fig. 8.

Distance from Buildings.—To secure the best results the distance at which trees are set from the building-line should

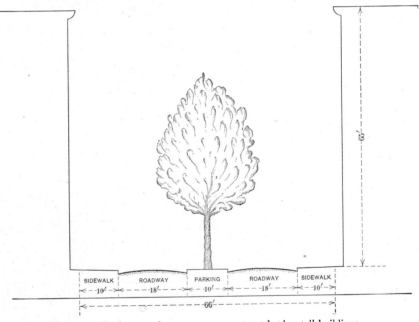

SIDEWALK   ROADWAY   PARKING   ROADWAY   SIDEWALK
<--10'-->   --18'--   --10'--   --18'--   <--10'-->
<----------------------66'---------------------->

FIG. 8.—Single row of trees on narrow street having tall buildings.

equal about half the height of the houses. In the city of
Paris no trees are planted on streets which have tall buildings and which have sidewalks less than thirteen feet wide
and roadways twenty feet wide.

It is sometimes possible, however, to secure fair results
even on narrow streets having tall buildings, by choosing a

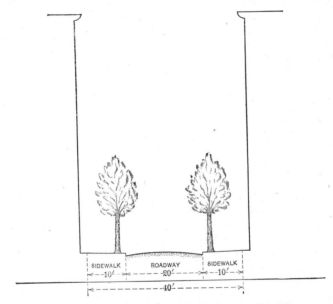

FIG. 9.—Small trees on a narrow street having tall buildings.

species that will keep small, or one that will permit of annual
heading back to small dimensions, as shown in Fig. 9.

Distance from Sidewalk Curb.—Trees should be set not
nearer than two feet from the curb, and, when the planting strips permit, it is better to put the trees farther away
from the curb than two feet. In resetting curbs, the roots
of trees must necessarily be cut, and if the trees are farther
away from the curb less injury is likely to result to them.

There is one phase of modern street-work that does not tend to improve the highway trees, and that is the laying of concrete walks. In order to lay these walks, there must be an excavation of about eighteen inches, and if there are old trees along the curb their roots are usually cut in the process. Flag walks should be preferred in such cases.

Frequently builders make it a practise to extend a strip of concrete of the width of the stoop of the house from the sidewalk to the curb. This is sometimes ten or twelve feet wide, and this encroachment on the parking space takes away still more from the possible nourishment of the tree, that is already severely hedged in by the curb on one side and the concrete walk on the other. It should be the desire of builders to make suburban streets as countrylike as possible, and not to extend these concrete strips.

Distance Apart of Specimens.—Even after the proper species has been selected there can be no greater mistake in street-planting than setting trees too close together. The distance between specimens should be such as to permit them to develop perfectly, and the outstretching limbs should not touch, even when the trees are fully grown. Forty feet is about the average distance at which street-trees should be set. The American elm should be set about fifty feet apart; the sugar maple, the red oak, the chestnut oak, and the oriental plane about forty-five feet apart; the Norway maple and the red maple about forty feet apart; the American linden and the pin oak about thirty-eight feet apart; the European linden, the sweet gum, and the horse-chestnut about thirty-five feet apart; the gingko, the catalpa, the hackberry about thirty feet apart; the ailantus and the Carolina poplar about twenty-eight feet apart.

It must also be remembered in determining the dis-

tance apart at which street-trees are to be set whether the
specimens are to be allowed to grow naturally, or whether
an attempt will be made to limit their spread. Thus, in the
city of Paris the spread of the trees is limited, and they are
kept rather small. Accordingly the distances above given
would be too far apart for the setting of its trees. In Paris,
therefore, the street-trees of the species above enumerated
are set at distances apart equal to about three-quarters or
less of the distances above given.

When planting is not done by public officials, nearly every
individual wants one or more trees in front of his house.
His neighbor has the same desire, irrespective of the frontage of his property or the nearness of other trees. Examples of the results of such methods of planting may be seen
on streets in any town. The trees are too close together,
frequently not more than twelve or fifteen feet apart. They
interfere with each other's growth, cut off the necessary
light and air, and prevent, by their shade, the growth of
grass under them. As a result the trees look like a thick
hedge and their individual beauty is lost. When the mistake
of having planted trees too close together is realized, one
frequently hears expressions of regret: "What a beautiful
street this would be, if those fine trees were ten or fifteen
feet farther apart."

Commonwealth Avenue, Boston, has been a notable
example of the crowding of street-trees, due to the lack of
foresight of the original planters. The planting-space on
this prominent thoroughfare is one hundred feet wide, and
the plans provided for the planting of four rows of American elms, the trees in the rows to stand opposite each other.
In 1880, Professor Charles Sprague Sargent and Frederick
Law Olmsted proposed the removal of the four rows of trees

which had already been planted between Arlington and Dartmouth Streets, and the planting in their place of two rows of trees from one end of the avenue to the other. The city government, however, refused to act on their suggestion. In 1880 and 1881, by order of the Common Council, the planting of four rows of trees was continued in this avenue up to Massachusetts Avenue. The Park Commissioners of Boston are now confronted with the problem of thinning out the trees.

Trees Set with Relation to the Street.—Trees should be set out with relation to each other and the street as a whole, and not with relation to the frontage of individual property. In the more recently developed sections of cities where property is high, single lots may range in width from twenty to thirty feet. The average distance required by shade-trees for proper development is from thirty-five to forty-five feet; hence there must necessarily be some houses that will not have trees in front of them. Fine shade-trees, however, benefit the entire street, and after they become large every house profits by them. When that time comes it matters little in front of which particular property the stem of the tree is located.

The Spacing Uniform.—The spacing of the trees should be uniform, and the specimens on the two sides of the street opposite each other. There will be many obstacles in the ordinary street, such as lamp-posts, water hydrants, house, water, and gas connections, that will prevent an absolutely uniform spacing of trees. Judgment will then have to be used as to how to redistribute the distance so that there will be least deviation from a uniform plan. Trees should be kept away at least eight feet from lamp-posts and about ten feet from water hydrants.

Opposite or Alternate.—On narrow walks and streets the plan of alternating the trees zigzag fashion on both sides of the way is found preferable, because the distance at right angles across the space is so small that the trees would interfere with each other's growth, but in the case of broad streets more effective results are obtained by placing the trees opposite each other.   By that method the trees at the intersection of the two streets are symmetrically disposed with respect to the four corners.

Treatment of Corners.—Exactly at a corner is a bad place for a tree, as that spot is usually reserved for a lamp-post, letter-box, fire-alarm box, catch basin, or other street fixture.   At a corner, also, a tree would be exposed to injury, and the curbstones, half surrounding it, would cut off a great deal of the nourishment from the soil.   The best arrangement for trees at street crossings, therefore, is to set them from twenty to twenty-five feet from the intersection of the curbs, so that there will be eight trees at every four corners, as shown in Fig. 10.

Setting Trees Between Sidewalk and Property-Line.— While the usual space reserved for tree-planting is the strip between the curb and the sidewalk, trees are sometimes set on the strip between the sidewalk and the property-line. Trees so located are not exposed to the injury of horses and passing vehicles.   The soil between the sidewalk and the property-line is also likely to be of better quality, and the trees will grow better.   Such plan of planting is to be preferred if the street roadway is rather narrow and the houses are set far back from the sidewalk.   If the houses are very near the fence-line it is evident that the trees will be too close to them and will shade them too much.   On the other hand, the roadway will get too little shade.   It is for these

reasons that in the great majority of cases the plan of planting shade-trees along the strip between the sidewalk and
the curb is followed. The sidewalk and the roadway get

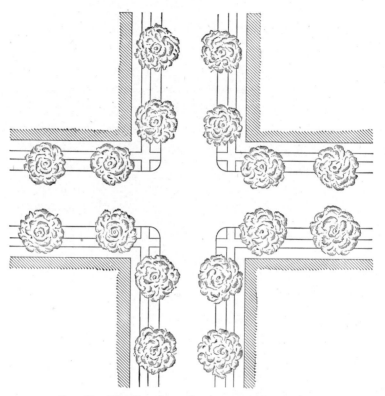

Fig. 10.—The disposition of trees at street intersections.

their fair share of shade and the trees are not too close to
the houses.

When sidewalks are placed next to the roadway, pedestrians are more likely to become spattered with dust and
mud than when protected by an intervening space. The
effect of a walk separated from the roadway by trees, which

give it a certain amount of seclusion, is also far better than that of a walk which exposes those using it to the continued gaze of passers-by.

Double Row.—Frequently a double row of trees is planted on the sidewalk—one row along the curb and a second row between the sidewalk and the property-line or immediately within the property-line and parallel with the street. Such a plan should be avoided. While the trees are small the result is likely to be effective, but within a few years after planting the trees begin to interfere with each other's growth, and the result is a bad crowding. The inside row of trees grows much more vigorously than the outside row, because it usually has better soil, and crowds the outside row and dwarfs its growth. The row of trees along the curb, however, is the more desirable; and if any trees are to be removed, those inside can be better spared. They are, as a rule, however, the better trees, and it is a difficult problem to decide which trees are to go if one wants to rectify the mistake of the original planter.

Number of Rows of Trees.—The total number of rows of trees that might be planted on a street depends upon the width of the highway, the width of the sidewalks or planting strips, and the species used. In the city of Paris an ordinance prescribes the planting of trees according to the following regulations:

Width of Highway.	Width of Roadway.	Width of Sidewalks.	Number of Rows of Trees.	Distance from Houses.	Distance from Roadway.
86 ft. to 92 ft.	40 ft.	23 ft. to 26 ft.	2	18 ft. to 21 ft.	5 ft.
100 ft. to 112 ft.	46 ft.	26 ft. to 33 ft.	2	21 ft. to 28 ft.	5 ft.
120 ft. to 125 ft.	40 ft. to 43 ft.	40 ft. to 41 ft.	4	16.5 ft. to 18 ft.	5 ft.
132 ft.	46 ft.	43 ft	4	21 ft.	5 ft.

ONE SPECIES ON A STREET

Not only to obtain variety but also to offset the whole-
sale spread of tree diseases, it is important that as many
good shade-trees as possible should be planted in a city. All
the specimens on a street, however, should be of the same
kind. When such a plan is followed there is secured increased stateliness, impressiveness, and charm. The beauty
and uniformity that are produced by a repetition of the
same object are lost when a mixture of species differing in
habits of growth and in foliage is introduced, and it is as
much at variance with good taste as would be a mixture of
orders in the columns of a temple.

Streets that have become famous for their beautiful
shade-trees, both in this country and abroad, are planted
with one variety. No better illustration of the effective
results of uniform planting can be found in America than
in the city of Washington. Some of the most imposing
streets are New Jersey Avenue, nearly three miles in length,
lined with four rows of American elms; Massachusetts
Avenue, three and a half miles in length, planted with
American lindens; Indiana Avenue, set with oriental planes,
and Pennsylvania Avenue, with pin oaks. In the capitals of
Europe the plan of planting one species of tree on a street is
also followed.

What Determines the Choice of Species.—The factors
which determine the choice of species for a particular
street are the width of the street, the nature of the soil,
particular local conditions and the general character of
the trees in a row as contributing to the beauty of the
street.

Rows of Different Species.—When the plantation consists of more than two parallel rows, highly decorative effects can be obtained by having the central rows of different species than the outside rows. These species may vary in character of growth, color of the foliage or flowers, so as to produce the most striking effects.

CHAPTER V

THE PLANTING OF STREET-TREES

THE TREE IN THE WOODS

AFTER the planting plan is complete the trees must be selected in the nursery. If in the woods you will pull a tree seedling out of the ground you will see that the downward or tap-root is almost as long as the stem. If left to grow, the root system of such a seedling would become as large as the top. If you wished to transplant it after a few years' growth, it would be difficult to take up all the roots; and if many of them were left behind, the tree would have a poor chance to live after transplanting. There is always a balance between the roots and the top of a tree. The cutting away of the roots will tend to retard the growth of the crown. Because of the risk attending the successful transplanting of trees from the woods, it is the practise in the planting of shade-trees to get all the specimens from a nursery.

THE TREE IN THE NURSERY

Developing of the Roots.—In the nursery the tree is trained to withstand the hardship of being transplanted to its final home. Seedlings a few feet high are dug up, the tap-roots are removed to within a few inches of the stem and set out in nursery rows, the rows being about five feet apart. The seedlings no longer send downward roots, but develop a lateral root system; just as when the leader of a

PLATE 21.—FROM THE NURSERY TO THE STREET.

1. Seedling in the woods, with long tap-root.   2. Seedlings of White Elm in nursery rows.   3. Fibrous root system of a 2½-inch nursery-grown Norway Maple. 4. Trees shipped in gondola-car.   5. Trees heeled-in.   6. Planting a Norway Maple.

tree is removed it sends out horizontal branches. After one or two years of growth the trees are again transplanted, and this time the ends of the lateral roots are shortened. As an additional means of preventing the spread of the roots, a plow is sometimes run between the nursery rows. In this manner the transplanting process is continued every year or two, and the roots, being prevented from spreading, develop a compact fibrous bundle near the stem. As a result, when the tree is finally moved to be set out on the street, it has all the roots necessary to supply the top.

Developing of the Stem.—In addition to the development of the root system the main stems of nursery-grown shade-trees are kept free from branches to a height of several feet from the ground by removing the lateral buds or small shoots. The upper twigs are shortened from time to time to produce a well-filled top.

Limitation of Size.—It is apparent that the processes outlined above cannot be continued indefinitely, and as a tree becomes larger less of the root system can be taken up on final transplanting. There is, therefore, a natural limitation to the size of the tree that may be most advantageously planted. A larger tree takes longer to recover from the loss of roots and makes little growth; while a smaller one continues its growth after transplanting with the least interruption. It is found that for general planting, trees from two inches and a half to three inches in diameter give the best results.

From an economic standpoint also the planting of large trees is impracticable. Trees of considerable size, seven or eight inches in diameter, set out with the care necessary in such cases, are very expensive; because the frequent transplantings of the trees in the nursery bring their final cost

1. A frozen mass of roots and earth, seven feet in diameter, has been liberated. By tilting the tree first to one side and then to the other, and putting soil underneath the root-mass, the trench is filled up and the roots brought above grade. 2. The trunk is then lashed to the rear truck of the tree-mover; planks are put under the wheels, and the tree raised. 3. The tree resting on the rear truck of the tree-mover. 4. The forward and the rear trucks are connected by a platform suspended by chains from the axles. The rear truck, with the tree, is backed up and the platform caught by the chains. The roots rest on the platform while the tree is being transported. (The tree-mover shown belongs to the Essex County, N. J., Park Commission.)

rather high. Of course in special cases, where an immediate effect is desired and the expense can be incurred, larger
trees may be planted with very good results. On the other
hand, if one plants an entire street, where perhaps few
houses have been built, it is clearly more economical to set
out small, thrifty trees that will grow to fair size by the
time the street will have been entirely improved.

Transplanting Large Specimens.—Very large trees, twelve
or fifteen inches in diameter, are sometimes successfully
transplanted. It is important in such cases to take up as
much of the root system as possible; and there are two processes of accomplishing that end. One method is to take up
the tree with a large ball of earth around the roots, ten or
twelve feet in diameter, and transport it to its new place.
This is best done when there is frost in the ground. Another
way is to dig a circular trench around the tree, about twenty
feet in diameter, work toward the stem by liberating the
fine rootlets and large roots, and then, by means of heavy
machinery, lift the entire tree and haul it to where it is
to be placed. Either of these processes is very expensive.
When a tree so transplanted is to be placed on a lawn, it
is possible to preserve all the roots; but it is evident that
if it were to be placed on a street all the roots would have
to be cut to accommodate it between the curb and the sidewalk, and the chances of its surviving the ordeal would be
very small. Besides, on a highway the tree would be a
source of danger, because of the loss of the anchor roots.

In the city of Paris, in order to maintain the uniformity
of plantations along the streets, when trees fifteen or twenty
years old die, they are replaced with specimens as nearly as
possible of the same size. To accomplish this successfully
the trees are trained for that in the municipal nursery. The

roots are cut round every three or four years by digging a circular trench around the base of the trees to prevent the elongation of the roots. By this means the root system is formed in a compact mass within a limited volume. The trees are transported from the nursery in heavy trucks especially constructed for the purpose.

Points in Selecting Trees.—In selecting a shade-tree a compact root system is of greater importance than a large top; although, of course, both are desirable. The abundant roots will cause rapid growth; but a large head and scant roots will result in little growth if the tree survives at all. The ideal street-tree must also have a straight stem, clear of branches to a height of at least seven feet from the ground and a well-defined leader.

It is always best to order trees from a nursery as near-by as possible. The less exposure of the roots from the time of digging to final transplanting the better for the tree. It is not always possible, however, to get desirable stock at a near-by place, and the planter may be obliged to go a considerable distance from home to select his trees. If proper precautions are taken in the digging, packing, shipping, unloading, and protection of the trees on arrival, the danger of loss is greatly reduced.

How Shipped.—The trees selected by the purchaser are marked and left in the nursery until the time of shipment. When digging, care is taken to get the entire root system. To insure the delivery of the trees in as perfect a condition as when they left the nursery they are carefully packed. If only a few trees constitute the order they are generally shipped in bales; the roots are packed in wet moss and burlapped, and the stems and branches are wrapped in straw. A hundred trees or more are shipped in a closed car. The trees are piled in rows and the roots are covered with wet straw and moss. The doors of the car being tightly closed the evaporation is reduced to a minimum, and the trees remain in good condition for one or two weeks. When too many trees are packed in a box car it is difficult to unload them without breaking some of the twigs. Hence it is better to ship four or five hundred trees in a gondola car with the sides and the roof built up of boards. The top of such car can be removed on arrival and the trees lifted out with absolutely no injury.

A Municipal Nursery.—Even with the greatest care exercised in digging, packing, and shipping stock from a nursery, the trees suffer a great deal from these hardships, and their chances to reestablish themselves when set out are not so good as when trees are grown in a municipal nursery, and can be dug and planted the same day. A municipal nursery is a necessary adjunct to a shade-tree department. When a nursery is controlled and operated by a city it is possible to get the quality of trees wanted. Their training from the seedling stage to the time when they are ready to be set out on the street is with the point in view of their use as street-trees. Their branching can be fixed at the proper height and the trees developed with single leaders. The trees from the municipal nursery are available whenever wanted, and they can be taken up and transplanted with all the roots and the least exposure. The cost of self-grown stock is also frequently much less than that purchased from a nursery.

It is also possible in a municipal nursery to keep in reserve large specimens of different species to take the place of any that die in the streets, and in that way the uniformity of the plantations can be maintained.

PRECAUTIONS IN PLANTING

Heeling-In.—So far in the history of the tree it has been out of the hands of the planter; but after its arrival success depends upon the protection of the roots, the preparation of the soil, and the careful planting. If the stock cannot be planted immediately on arrival it should be "heeled-in." This is done by digging a trench about a foot and a half deep, and of sufficient width to accommodate the roots of the trees without bending. In this trench the trees are set close together and the roots covered with soil, care being taken that it is well worked in about them so as not to leave vacant spaces. Trees so protected can be kept for some weeks, and a few planted at a time as the holes are ready.

Top and Root Pruning.—Before setting the tree, a few points are to be observed. Since even with the greatest care it is impossible to take up all the roots when transplanting a tree, it is necessary to cut back the top to maintain the balance with the roots. The amount of cutting depends on the condition of the roots; the more fibrous they are the less the necessity of reducing the top. It is a good rule to remove about four-fifths of last year's growth from all the branches, making a clean cut just above some strong bud. This can be done more easily and rapidly before the trees are planted. All broken roots should be carefully trimmed to enable them to heal.

The amount of top-pruning also depends upon the species, as not all trees transplant with the same ease. The soft maples, planes, elms, and poplars, for example, do not require as severe pruning as the oaks, the magnolias, or the sweet gum. It must be borne in mind, however, that it is better to prune more than not enough. In a year or two the trees recover by rapid growth the loss of the shortening of the branches. New shoots begin close to the stem, and the trees form a compact top. If a tree is not cut back sufficiently when transplanted, if it survives at all, the foliage is thin and borne only on the ends of the branches. Figs. 11,

Fig. 11.—Young Sugar Maple before tree has been top-pruned.

Fig. 12.—Same Sugar Maple after being top-pruned, preparatory to setting out.

12, and 13 will suggest about the way in which trees should be top-pruned. Fig. 12 will serve as an example of top-pruning such species as maples, elms, planes, and lindens. Fig. 13 will serve as an illustration for such trees as the oaks, magnolias, and sweet gum.

How the Tree is Set.—The tree is set the same depth it

stood in the nursery, and the roots are spread naturally, without twisting or crowding them. Fine soil is sifted over the roots and carefully worked between and under them, so that no spaces remain unfilled. A pointed stick helps to crowd the soil under and around them. The soil is filled by layers and packed with the feet until within about three or four inches of the top. The last of the soil is thrown loosely on top, so that it acts as a mulch and helps to retain the moisture.

When to Plant.—A question frequently raised in tree-planting is: When is the best time to plant, in the spring or in the fall? The problem will be better understood if some of the points in tree-growth are mentioned. During the summer—the period of growth—there is a constant demand on the roots to supply the top of the tree. Fatal injury would result to the tree if an attempt were made to transplant it at that time, as the leaves would immediately dry. From the time of the falling of the leaves in the autumn to the swelling of the buds in the spring is the period of rest, and it is during that time, in the dormant state, that trees may be safely moved.

Fig. 13.—Pin Oak, top pruned ready for planting.

Theoretically the best time to transplant trees would be after the leaves have fallen—about the end of October or the beginning of November. The trees would then be ready to resume growth the following spring. Practically, however, the best results are not always obtained in fall planting.

Work in the fall is most successful when the following winter is mild and a heavy mulching of manure is placed on the ground at the base of the tree. One of the dangers of fall-planting is the upheaval of the tree by the freezing and the thawing of the ground.

It is seldom that trees planted in the fall make new roots before the ground freezes. In the meantime the evaporation of moisture from the trunk and branches goes on; the roots likewise suffer, so that the tree is not in so good a state as if it had been allowed to remain in the nursery and transplanted in the latter part of March or early April. At that time it would be perfectly healthy; and, as growth would begin, new roots would start to form. Of course, there is danger in spring-planting of the unfolding leaves making too great a draft on the roots for sap and moisture that is not always supplied by rain. Artificial watering is then necessary to carry the tree over the critical period of transplanting, which at best is a severe shock to the tree.

Experience has shown that trees planted in the fall, if they come up in the spring at all, grow very slowly, unfolding their leaves later than trees of the same stock coming from the same nursery planted in the following spring. While a good deal depends on weather conditions, it may be said that the fall is not a bad season to plant, but the spring is a much better one, provided the trees are planted before the buds begin to swell. Certain trees which have succulent roots, like the tulip-tree, sweet gum, and magnolias, cannot be transplanted successfully in the autumn at all.

The difficulty in spring-planting is that the season is very short. Everybody is rushed, and trees are sometimes not handled so carefully as the longer fall-planting season permits. From the natural consideration, however, of the tree's growth, better success is obtained by careful spring work.

STAKING

One of the elements of beauty in the planting of shade-trees, is to have them perfectly vertical. In spite of the greatest care in planting, the settling of the earth and the swaying of the trees in the wind cause them to get out of vertical. Attempts to straighten the trees from time to time disturb the roots and injure the tree. The staking of trees, therefore, is an absolute necessity to keep them straight until their roots take firm hold of the ground.

An elaborate but effective device for holding the trees upright after being planted is employed in Washington, shown in Plate 23, Fig. 3. This consists of a four-sided wooden box around each tree, which is nailed to four stakes driven into the ground. The trees are fastened by means of leather straps to each corner of the box and are kept perfectly vertical. The boxes, which also serve as guards, are retained for eight or ten years until the trees outgrow them. They are then removed and wire netting is put around the trees to protect them from injury.

Single Stake.—It must be borne in mind that in every device designed to keep young trees upright there must be provision made to keep the top from swaying and bending over as well as keeping the stem rigid at a height of six or seven feet from the ground. Oriental planes, and oaks especially, have a tendency to bend over on account of their weight of foliage, and sometimes the tops snap off in a wind. It has been found, therefore, that one long stake is the best thing to use to support young trees.

PLATE 23.—GUARDING AND STAKING.

1. Guarding and staking of trees in East Orange. Guard is of No. 16, ½-inch square wire mesh, seven inches in diameter and six feet high, stake is fifteen feet long, driven to depth of three feet. 2. Good guard for large trees, made of No. 16, 2-inch hexagonal wire mesh. 3. Guarding and staking device used in Washington, D. C. 4. Making hole with crowbar for stake. End of tarred stake on the ground is seen. 5. Driving stake. An 18-foot "A" ladder is used.

Stakes fifteen feet long are used which are driven to a depth of three feet, thus leaving twelve feet above ground. The tree is tied to the stake at two or three places by means of one-fourth inch Manila rope slipped through a piece of three-quarter inch rubber hose, Plate 23, Fig. 1. The pieces of hose are about eight or nine inches long. The rope is slipped through them, is wrapped around the tree and a double knot is tied, then the ends of the rope are tied around the stake. In that way the stem of the tree does not come in contact with the stake. If only possible, the stake is driven on the side of the tree contrary to the direction of the prevailing winds, so that the tree will be blown away from the stake and chafing will be minimized.

The stakes should not be of sawn lumber but of young growth, about three and one-half inches at the bottom and two inches at the top. To make the stakes more durable, they should be tarred to a distance of about four feet from the bottom. Stakes usually rot at the ground level. By leaving them tarred a foot above ground this will be prevented. The bark should be removed to the required distance and the stakes covered with molten pitch.

The stakes are placed about ten inches from the base of the tree. When tree-guards of small diameter are used, the stakes may be placed on the outside; or, if the guards permit it, the supports may be inside. To drive the stake easily a hole is made in the ground with a crowbar, flaring out at the bottom to a cross-section of about two inches square and terminating in a sharp point. The stakes are driven with a sledge hammer, "A" ladders, eighteen feet high, being used by the workmen to get up to the required height, as shown in Plate 23, Figs. 4 and 5.

GUARDING

The combination support and tree-guard used in the city of Washington has already been spoken of. While rather clumsy, these guards are very efficient, and remain around the trees for eight or nine years. Some forms of iron guards are used in other cities, which are rather expensive. Unless a tree is exposed to continuous and severe injury a cheaper form of wire guard will be found just as serviceable, especially on residential streets.

There are many tree-guards on the market with which trees can be protected. A good economical guard for young trees has been adopted by the East Orange Shade-Tree Commission. It is made of No. 16, one-half inch square wire mesh, coming in rolls twenty inches wide. It is cut into six-foot lengths, and these are rolled by means of a machine into cylinders. A good guard for trees of any size is made of hexagonal wire netting six or seven feet high. In the case of larger guards the width of the wire cloth ordered should be the same as the required height of the guard. The amount of wire cut off from the roll will depend upon the diameter of each tree protected.

GRILLS

Grills are used around the base of trees along streets to prevent the soil from being tramped on by pedestrians. They are especially needed on sidewalks covered with concrete or other material impervious to air and moisture, and where every available bit of room is necessary for the public use of the street.

They are circular, hexagonal, or rectangular in form, and are made of cast-iron sections set together around the

PLATE 24.—GUARDS AND GRILLS.

1. Guard and circular grill, Webster Avenue, New York. 2. Guards and rectangular grills, row of Norway Maples, Rutherford Place, New York. 3. Form of guard used by the Department of Parks, Bronx Borough, New York. 4. Guard and rectangular grill, Baird Court, New York Zoological Garden (*Photo. by Hermann W. Merkel, Forester of the Garden*). 5. Railing around base of trees on West Fifty-Ninth Street, New York. A railing is excellent if the sidewalk room can be spared. The soil within can be kept loose and the trees watered, mulched, and fertilized.

tree. They are placed on a level with the pavement and are supported by wooden pins driven in the ground. The soil under the grill is left depressed or basin-shaped, the deepest portion being that farthest from the base of the tree. This

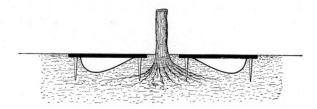

Fig. 14.—Method of placing grill. The soil beneath is left depressed.

depression of the soil affords a means of watering the trees. The soil immediately around the trunk is left at grade. See Fig. 14.

SUBIRRIGATION

The installation of a system of subirrigation becomes necessary to permit the watering of trees by sending the water directly to the soil through tile pipes. This usually consists of tile pipes about three inches in diameter, placed with open joints at a depth of about a foot or a foot and a half. A branch pipe, carried up to the surface of the ground, furnishes an inlet to water delivered to the tree from a water-cart or a hydrant hose. The drains are laid either in the form of a rectangle surrounding the tree, or simply in a straight line on one side of the tree, as shown in Figs. 15 and 16. In either case there is a branch pipe for the admission of the water.

A cast-iron cap may be used to cover the opening at the top of the branch pipe to prevent clogging with soil. To guard against any tampering with the irrigation device, the top of the branch pipe may end slightly below the surface of the ground, the opening covered with a cap, and the soil brought to grade. When watering, the soil is stirred aside and the cap lifted, and when through the cap is again re-placed and covered with soil so as not to show on the outside.

The ground in which the tree is planted must be thor-

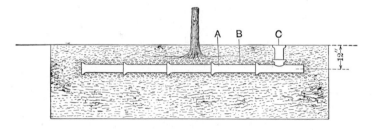

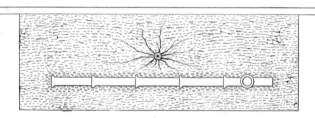

Fig. 15. —Sectional view and plan of a subirrigation device of 4-inch tile pipes laid with open joints. A, Tile pipe. B, Layer of broken stone. C, Branch pipe.

oughly settled before the drain is placed. Then a channel is dug for the drain and the tile pipes are laid perfectly level and separated from the earth by a layer of broken stone or coarse gravel three or four inches in thickness. This inter-mediary layer is necessary to facilitate the flow of water and to prevent the soil from washing into the drain.

Such irrigation devices are costly and are not always efficient. They become clogged with soil and roots of the growing trees, and in a short time are no longer serviceable. There is nothing better for the welfare of trees than the planting of them in such a way as to make it possible to loosen the soil around the roots and water them from the

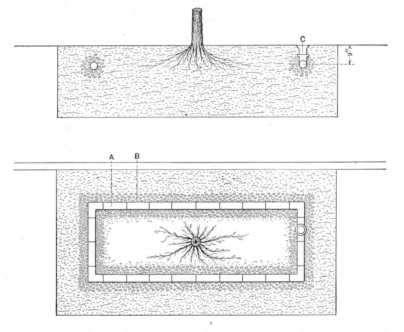

FIG. 16.—Sectional view and plan of subirrigation device of 3-inch perforated agricultural tile. A, Perforated tile. B, Layer of broken stone. C, Branch pipe and cap.

surface. If grills are used, they can be removed from time to time, the soil loosened, and then the watering done through the grills.

DRAINAGE OF SUBSOIL

What is absolutely essential to the welfare of a tree is proper subsoil drainage. It does not matter how good the soil may be, or how much care has been exercised in the selection and planting of a tree, if the water table is so low that the roots are always moist and there is no access of air to it, the tree will die.   Proper subsoil drainage frequently presents one of the most insuperable problems in tree-planting.   If the soil is of an impervious nature, but limited in thickness, it should be either dug through to the more pervious soil or a drain carried to the lower stratum.   A drain connecting with a street-sewer will also serve to carry off water that is likely to collect at the roots.   Such drains should be placed at a depth of from three and one-half to four feet.

CHAPTER VI

THE CARE OF STREET-TREES

HOW A TREE GROWS

Evolution of a Tree.—Success in the care of trees necessarily depends upon the knowledge of their requirements to maintain life and their mode of growth. Let us, therefore, for a moment trace the evolution of a tree. The tree's beginning is long before it becomes established in the soil, and shows the differentiating parts of root system, stem, and crown. Its birth really occurs on the parent-tree from which the seed comes. The seed contains the rudiments of all the parts of the mature tree.

The Seedling.—In Plate 25, Fig. 4, is shown a common lima bean dissected. The thick fleshy parts, which form the initial leaves on germination, are called cotyledons. These are attached to the very short initial stem. Below that is the initial root, which on germination turns downward and penetrates into the soil. As the root continues its growth, the stem adds to its length, and, in seeking the light, brings the seed up out of the ground. In the case of the lima bean the cotyledons become the first pair of leaves. Many seeds of trees germinate in the same way.

In the case of the seeds of other trees, as the white maple, for example, the cotyledons are not lifted out of the soil and transformed into actual leaves. The growth below the cotyledons is nearly all root. The rudimentary bud between

PLATE 25.—GUARD-ROLLING MACHINE. SEEDLINGS. WATERING-CART.

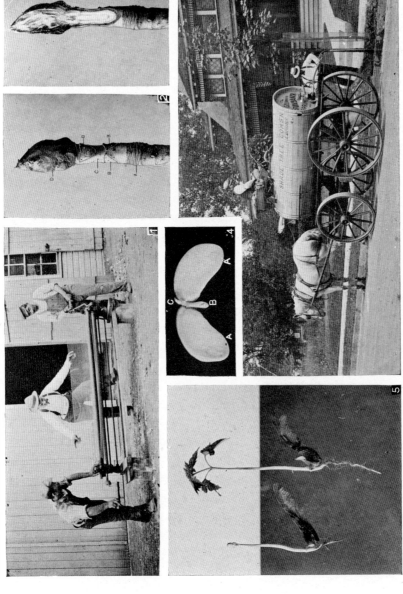

1. A machine for rolling wire guards, used by the East Orange Shade-Tree Commission. 2. Winter twig of Horse-chestnut: A, Budscale scars; B, B, B, Leaf scars; C, Lenticel; D, Terminal bud. The growth in height during the preceding summer was from A to the top of the terminal bud. 3. Section of the Horse-chestnut bud, showing the rudimentary twig within. 4. Lima-bean dissected: A, A, Cotyledons; B, Caulicle, which forms the roots; C, Plumule, which forms the leaves. 5. Germinating seeds of White Maple. The wings of the fruit are only for the purpose of dissemination by the wind. 6. Watering-cart used by the East Orange Shade-Tree Commission. Water is discharged through a ⅜-inch hose. Note trough made before watering.

them makes the upward growth of stem and leaves. The materials for the growth are supplied by the cotyledons or seed leaves. The seedling, although diminutive and most simple, possesses all the organs of the fully developed tree; namely, roots in the soil, the stem rising out of it, and the leaves in the light and open air. It now draws in moisture and food materials from the soil by its roots, conveys them through the stem into the leaves, where these materials together with the other crude food which the leaves imbibe from the air, are assimilated into growing tissue.

Growth in Height.—In the autumn, after the leaves have fallen from the seedling, the bare stem represents the height and thickness of the first season's growth. If the seedling is carefully examined, it is seen that just above the points where the leaves were attacked during the growing season are the buds, from which the growth of stems and leaves will be continued. The shoot from the terminal bud will prolong the height of the central stem, and the lateral buds will form the branches. Growth in height ceases for the season as soon as the shoot develops from the bud, and this is usually indicated when the terminal leaves are fully grown. The tree adds no other way to the length of limb and trunk.

There is a general impression that trees add to their height by the gradual lengthening of the trunks and limbs. If this were true, nails driven into the trunk one above the other, would gradually become farther apart, and wire fences nailed to trees would rise in the air.

Growth in Diameter.—While the growth of a tree in height is the result only of the shoots developing from the buds, the growth in diameter of the trunk, main branches, and twigs is a process affecting every part of the entire plant.

Separating the bark from the wood is a colorless, mucilaginous substance called the cambium layer. The cambium is under every portion of the bark, which covers the tree completely from the tip of the deepest root to the top of the highest twig. Through the sapwood the soluble inorganic materials drawn from the soil by the roots ascend to the leaves, and are there elaborated in connection with the materials taken from the air into organized compounds. This elaborated food material descends through the cambium layer to every part of the plant to build up its tissues. All the tissue arising from the inner side of the cambium ring goes to form the wood, while that produced on the outside goes to make up the bark.

The cambium is the life of the tree. If the limb of a tree is removed, a new one may develop near its place. Trees live for years with the trunks hollow, but if they are girdled by the cutting away of a ring of bark, there is interrupted the tissue through which the descending food material is conducted from the leaves, and the roots are starved and the tree dies.

Owing to the climatic variations during the growing season, the cambium tissue is not uniformly active. During the spring, the period of energetic growth, wood of a coarser texture is deposited than later in the season, when it is more closely grained. Through the contrast in the structure of the early and the late wood, the limits between successive annual rings become sharply defined and serve as a means of computing the age of a tree.

Essentials for Normal Growth.—The food of trees comes from two sources—the air and the soil. The tree can transform the raw materials into wood tissue only under the proper conditions of soil, water, light, air, and climate. Water serves the double purpose of keeping in solution the minerals taken up by the roots, and helps to convey these nutrient substances of the soil into the tree body. A large quantity of the water taken up by the roots passes through the tree merely as a medium for the transport of nourishment, and is again discharged through the leaves by evaporation. This evaporation of water through the leaves is called transpiration.

The watery fluid absorbed by the roots is carried by the transpiration current to the leaves. These in turn take up the carbonic acid from the air, and under the action of sunlight the carbonic acid is decomposed, the carbon combined with the minerals from the soil into food materials used in building up the tree. This process is called assimilation. The leaves, therefore, perform a very vital function in the life of the tree, and it is evident that defoliation by insects or other causes will seriously affect its growth.

Besides, trees, like animals, in order to live must have air to breathe, and in this process of respiration they take up oxygen and give off carbonic acid. Respiration and assimilation are two distinct vital processes, carried on independently by trees and other plants. The process of assimilation is carried on only in the light, carbonic acid is decomposed, and oxygen given off. The process of respiration is carried on both by day and by night, oxygen is taken up, and carbonic acid given off. Furthermore, not only the leaves but the twigs, the branches, the trunk, and the roots have breathing pores, and require air for the maintenance of life.

It will, therefore, be seen how important it is to keep the soil in a state of culture, and to see that the supply of air is not cut off from the roots by pavements, by filling in around the base, or by flooding of the roots.

Reserve Material.—All the products of assimilation are not at once consumed by the tree, but some are accumulated for future use. This surplus of reserve material is greatest at the close of the growing season in the fall. It is stored by the tree during the winter, and all growth of buds and leaves of the succeeding spring is dependent upon this store of elaborated food.

WATERING

Artificial watering of trees is necessary when they do not get by natural means the moisture essential to maintain the soil in a condition most favorable to vegetation. In cities the water from rainfall runs off quickly, and very little finds its way into the soil and subsoil around the roots of trees where it is most needed. Watering depends upon the climate, species of tree, and the nature and extent of the soil and subsoil. Young trees need more frequent watering than older ones. Trees that have surface roots need more watering than deeply rooted ones; also rapidly growing trees more so than those of slow growth.

Especially after transplanting, when they begin to reestablish themselves and during their first season's growth, trees need an abundance of water. Before the trees are able to care for themselves, new roots must be formed to take hold of the soil. In the meantime the evaporation from the branches and the developing leaves must be supplied artificially.

How Much Water.—How much water to give trees, and at what intervals, depend upon the extent of soil occupied by the roots and the nature of the soil and subsoil. Young trees, two or three years after planting, of which the roots occupy a volume of about a cubic yard, require from twenty to twenty-five gallons at every watering. Older trees require more water. It must always be borne in mind that enough water should be used to penetrate the soil in which the roots of the tree extend. Watering at intervals of every week or ten days will, on the average, be found sufficient if every time the soil around the roots is thoroughly saturated. While on the one hand there must be enough watering to maintain a uniform degree of moisture in the soil, on the other hand care must be taken not to allow too much moisture around the roots.

How to Water.—When watering is provided for by a system of subirrigation of tile pipes, the process is simple, as the necessary quantity of water can be supplied through the branch pipe carried to the surface. When there is no such provision made for watering, the soil around the base of the tree should be thoroughly loosened and a shallow basin formed around the tree about eight inches deep. The size of this basin will depend upon the extent of the roots of the trees desired to water. Ordinarily the extent of the roots of trees is about the same diameter as that of the crown. The deepest part of the basin should be the portion farthest away from the stem of the tree. When trees have grills, the soil underneath should be left depressed in the form of a basin, to permit of watering.

The water is applied from a hydrant or from a watering-cart, and is allowed to run slowly, so that all of it will soak into the soil. Before the soil hardens and packs, the loose soil that was removed to form the basin should be replaced, and the ground brought to grade. By keeping the soil porous the moisture is retained for a longer period of time. In the city of Paris watering devices, covered with grills, are installed in the intermediary spaces between very large trees, the root systems of which have become very extensive. Watering of trees should be avoided during the hottest part of the day. It is best to do it in the early morning and late in the afternoon or evening. In the city of East Orange the watering of the street-trees is done at night, from 7 P.M. to 6 A.M.

CULTIVATING AND FERTILIZING

The principal elements in the soil essential to plant growth are nitrogen, phosphoric acid, and potash. It is generally found in cities that it is not the deficiency of the nutritive elements in the soil that causes the decline of trees, but rather the physical condition of the soil which renders it impossible for trees to perform their normal functions. The keeping of the soil around trees cultivated and free from weeds is one of the most important aids to their growth. The keeping of the ground loose allows air to reach the roots, renders more available the plant food the soil contains, and prevents the rapid evaporation of moisture. If the ground is hard it becomes heated, the water forces itself to the surface, and passes into the atmosphere. If kept cultivated it acts like a blanket, and prevents the loss of water by surface evaporation.

Too much stress cannot be laid upon the importance of cultivation, the full value of which is not generally appreciated. When there is no water available, trees can frequently be brought through in good condition during a period of drought by just keeping the soil dug up and loose around their base.

One of the best ways of improving the condition of the soil of trees is to put a mulching of manure around them in the fall, allow that to remain all winter, and then turn the manure into the soil the following spring. The manure not only enriches the soil chemically, but improves its physical condition by making it more porous and less liable of becoming packed and impervious to air and moisture. In the case of young trees this treatment is especially beneficial.

Instead of manure, chemical fertilizers can be used very advantageously, to stimulate the trees in their growth. The following mixture is recommended by Dr. Jacob G. Lipman, soil chemist of the New Jersey Agricultural Experiment Station:

Acid phosphate....................700 pounds
Muriate of potash.................300 pounds

The above mixture is used in the fall at the rate of about fifteen hundred pounds per acre of ground. Proportionately the amount is determined for each tree according to the area it is desired to fertilize. In the succeeding spring the fertilizing is continued by an application of nitrate of soda at the rate of 300 pounds to the acre. The latter can be best applied by dissolving the chemical in water and then sprinkling the solution over the area to be fertilized.

TRAINING AND PRUNING

In the shaping and pruning of shade-trees, one is largely governed by the same points as when selecting a tree for planting. A lawn-tree may branch low or may be crooked and unsymmetrical. The very imperfections give it its character. The tree requires very little attention, and is left to grow naturally. A street-tree, on the other hand, must be perfectly straight, symmetrical, and the branches must begin at a height from the ground that will allow the free public use of the street.   Besides, the tree must have a well-developed, compact head, as nearly as possible of oval outline.   Many of the requisites of the good tree will be obtained by selecting the proper species for planting. To produce symmetry, good outline, and branching at a fixed height from the ground are the functions of training and pruning.

Fixing Height of Branching.—The training of the tree should begin soon after planting.   The fixing of the branching at a certain height above the ground must be done gradually, however.   It is desirable that a tree should grow in diameter as well as in height in order to support the top without bending.   Low branching will cause a more rapid growth in thickness.   The lower layers of branches should be removed at intervals of a year or more until the proper height of clean stem, ten or twelve feet, is reached.

Forming the Crown.—The training of the crown consists in shaping it for symmetry by the suppression of some branches and the encouragement of the growth of others. If possible, trees should be left with single leaders.   Two or three main stems produce crotches which are likely to split in later years.   When there is a tendency to the formation of two or more main stems, the central stem should be left and the others entirely removed, or so shortened that the entire vigor of growth will be thrown into the central stem. In the case of young oaks and other species of trees, of which the wood is very flexible, the leaders have a tendency to bend over, and the tops in time become drooping.   In such cases the leaders should be tied to bamboo poles of about an inch or an inch and a quarter in diameter.   Raffia is one of the best materials to use in tying trees to bamboo poles.   When a tree loses its leader, it can be made to resume the growth of a central stem by tying a lateral twig to a bamboo pole and training it upward for a few years.

The training of street-trees when young saves a great deal of work when the trees become older, when they do not lend themselves so readily to the process of shaping, and it is necessary to form large scars by removing large branches.

The Street as a Unit.—Very frequently, however, it is found necessary to prune trees of considerable age, and certain principles have to be borne in mind. As in the planting of shade-trees the street is treated as a unit, so in the pruning, each tree must be considered in relation to the others on the street. All trees should be trimmed to a height that will allow the unimpeded passage of pedestrians and vehicles. No limbs or foliage should be left to obstruct the street-lights. The shading of lamps is a trouble very common on many streets. The limbs are so low that the entire light is shut off at night, and the street is left in darkness.

No matter how healthy and perfect shade-trees may be, if the limbs are too low the full beauty of the street is not realized. In walking you may not actually be obliged to stoop in order to keep clear of the leaves; but there is a depressing effect produced by looking down the street and seeing the branches and the sidewalk almost meet. The foliage seems to oppress you with its density. The individuality of the trees is frequently lost, and the trees look like a great overgrown hedge. On the other hand, if one comes to a street the trees of which are properly pruned on both sides to a uniform height, the ends of the limbs turning upward instead of drooping, one cannot help perceive the improvement. The depressed effect is gone and one looks up. Every tree, instead of seeming like one mass of foliage, shows a prominent trunk, and the branching is clearly brought out. The perspective of the street resembles a great archway. Nothing of the health or utility of the trees has been sacrificed; and from an esthetic standpoint the maximum effect has been obtained. Contrast the appearance of the street shown in Fig. 17, and that shown in Plate 3.

FIG. 17.—A street the trees of which are in need of pruning.

Plate 3 shows Midland Avenue in East Orange, after the sugar maples were trimmed. Fig. 17 shows the continuation of the same street in Glen Ridge, where the pruning was stopped. The former street shows all the lamps, the branches turn upward and every tree stands out clearly. Fig. 17 shows the drooping limbs forming one mass of foliage that reaches almost to the ground.

The Individual Tree.—In the actual treatment of each

individual tree, great care and judgment are necessary. No two trees have their mode of branching alike, and each case must be studied separately before deciding what limbs are to go in order that the tree may be improved. No branch should be removed from a tree without good reason.

There are some points to be observed, however, that are applicable to all trees. All dead and imperfect limbs should be removed. The top of a tree should not be allowed to become so extremely dense as to exclude the sun from the soil or from the buildings near-by, or interfere with the free circulation of air. The tops of sugar maples and red maples particularly have a tendency to become too thick. To thin out the tops of such trees, the main limbs and the branches immediately radiating from them should best be left, and all cutting limited to the third and fourth divisions in the branching. In that way the character of the tree is not changed. Also in the removing of the lower branches of a tree that interfere with the public use of the street or obstruct street-lights, it is not necessary to clear the main trunk of limbs to a very great height; but subdivisions can be removed, giving the branches a graceful upward turn. The ends of the branches can be shortened. In that way the prime object in the pruning of shade-trees, to secure the unobstructed use of the street, is accomplished, and the natural habit of the trees is preserved.

In fact, the point to be constantly borne in mind in the pruning of shade-trees is to preserve, as far as possible, the character, natural shape, and habit of growth of each tree, and to avoid all artificial shaping of trees. The art of pruning consists of making the finished tree look as if no limbs had been removed at all.

How Best to Prune.—The work of pruning should begin

at the top of the tree, be continued in a downward direction, and completed at the bottom. It is easier to shape the tree by that method, and time is saved in clearing the tree of the pruned limbs. Frequently a limb gets caught in its fall; but as the man works downward he is able to free the limbs and do the cutting at the same time. All cuts should be made close to the base of a limb, and the plane of the scar should be nearly parallel to the axis of the trunk. How to make the cut to prevent splitting and to insure the healing of the scar are the important points in the pruning of all trees.

Origin of Branch.—A branch of a tree originates from a lateral bud of the main stem. The first year's growth of the shoot from the bud is similar to the first year's growth of the seedling from the seed. As the growth continues and the annual layers of wood are deposited on the main stem, the draft of the sap of the lateral shoot causes these layers to continue up and around the limb. If one were to stand and hold his arms up, the garments around his body would represent the successive annual layers of wood on the tree-trunk, and the sleeves of these garments around the arms would represent the continuation of these layers around the limbs of the trees.

The Wrong Way.—In Plate 26, Fig. 1, is shown the trunk of a tree with a limb that is to be removed. Frequently such work is done by making a cut the shortest way across the limb, line AB, Plate 26, Fig. 1, and the result is that a stub is left, similar to that shown in Plate 26, Fig. 2. When the limb is so removed, let us see what will happen. There being no draft of sap into the stub, because the end is removed, the next annual layer of wood of the main trunk will not be continued up around the limb, but will end at

PLATE 26.—THE EVOLUTION OF A KNOT-HOLE.

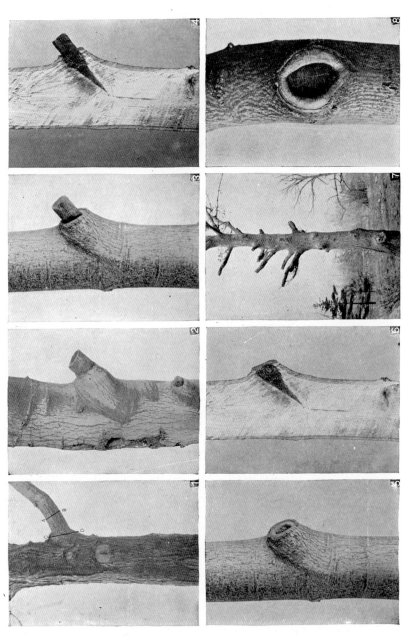

1. Limb is removed along the line AB. 2. Stub is left. 3. Bark falls away, tissue is deposited at base. 4. Section of same showing decay. 5. Stub falls out, leaving knot-hole. 6. Section showing that decay is carried far into the tree. 7. An example of years had running. 8. Healing of a running scar properly made.

the base of the stub, as shown in Plate 26, Fig. 2. The stub of wood being no longer living tissue and exposed to the weather, will dry, check, lose its bark, and the successive annual layers deposited on the trunk will form a collar at the base of the stub, as shown in Plate 26, Fig. 3.

In Plate 26, Fig. 4, which is a section of the specimen in the former figure, is shown the result of such a method of pruning. The decay caused by the stub has been carried to the heart of the tree. As time goes on the stub further rots, and breaks off at the collar, forming an ugly knot-hole, Plate 26, Fig. 5. Knot-holes resulting from improper pruning are very numerous. They form an admirable spot for the germination of fungus spores and the entrance of borers, and are frequently the first cause of the serious injury and final death of trees.

The Right Way.—Returning to Plate 26, Fig. 1, suppose the limb had been cut off close to the trunk, along the line CD, as far as possible parallel with the axis of the tree. Separating the wood from the bark is the cambium layer. All the tissue arising from the inner side of the cambium layer goes to form the wood, while the outside produces the bark. When a limb is cut off, as in Plate 26, Fig. 1, along the line CD, the living cells of the cambium bordering on the wound put forth an abnormal growth of tissue, called a callus. It first arises from the exposed cambium, like a thin ring, as shown in Plate 26, Fig. 8. With the growth of the tree it rolls over the scar and finally overcaps it.

How the Wound Heals.—While the callus tissue is in the process of overgrowing the wounded surface, it forms a protective bark and a new cambium under it, which is continuous with the cambium of the growing stem. When the margins of the overgrowing callus tissue meet, the edges of

PLATE 27.—THE HEALING OF A PRUNING-SCAR.

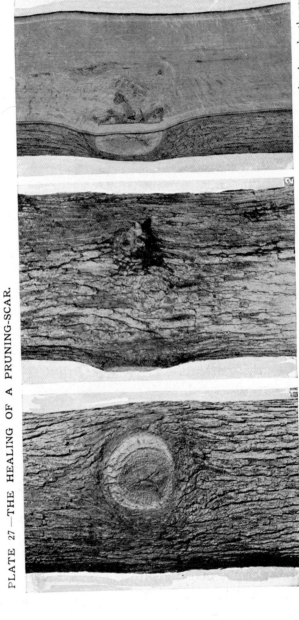

1. White Oak, showing front view of a completely healed pruning-scar. 2. Side view of the same, showing why the scar healed so nicely; the cut was made close to and even with the trunk. 3. A longitudinal section of the tree through the scar, slightly turned so as to show the exterior of the healing tissue. The stub A is seen overcapped by this tissue.

the cambium unite and form a complete layer over the surface of the wound. This layer is a continuation of the cambium of the growing stem, and during the next season a layer of growth will be added over the wound continuous with the annual ring added to the tree. The wood produced over wounds differs in structure from normal wood and is called callus wood. Eventually, however, the successive layers become more like natural wood.

The callus overgrowing the end of a severed branch never coalesces with the old wood. It simply seals up the remaining stub of the branch, which becomes like so much dead material buried in the wood of the tree. Fig. 18 and Plate 27, Fig. 3, show the transverse and the longitudinal sections of healed wounds caused by the removal of branches. It will be seen that the stubs remained exactly in the same condition as when the limbs were cut off, and that the layers of tissue of the subsequent growth of the trees have overcapped them.

Fig. 18.—Transverse section through callus on a horse-chestnut, showing stub A overcapped by tissue.

The importance of the proper healing of wounds cannot be overestimated. As has been pointed out before, limbs of trees originate in many cases from the very centre of the tree-trunks. After a limb is removed the remaining stub, which becomes lifeless, is like a cylindrical block of wood driven into the tree with the end exposed to the weather. If nature did not provide for the healing of the wound, or rather its overgrowing with new tissue, the stub would form a soil for fungus spores and the entrance of insects, and

the decay would be carried to the centre of the tree. It will
be seen, therefore, that it is extremely necessary when
removing a limb to make the cut in such a way as to aid

FIG. 19.—Tree with branch to   FIG. 20.—Split caused by improper
be removed along line A B.   method of pruning.

nature to heal the wound as effectively and as rapidly as
possible.

The way to do this is to make the cut as close as possible
to the base of the limb, and in a way that the plane of the
scar is nearly parallel with the axis of the tree. Two purposes are served by such a method: the wound is brought
into the most intimate contact with the healing tissues, and

the wood being deeper, there is less danger from drying and checking while the wound is healing.

Limb Must Not Split.—The necessity of making the cut, as described above, being apparent, the question now coming up is how to make the proper cut. In removing the branch in Fig. 19, the cut would have to be made along the line AB. If one were to start the cut with a saw at A, the weight of the limb would cause it to split when near the end of the cut, and the injury caused by the stripping of the bark would be very great. A safe way, perhaps, of removing the limb would be to cut it off about two feet from the shoulder, and then remove the stub. While it would be a safe way, it would not be the easiest or the most practicable way. The green wood across the junction of two branches is very tough, in which the saw binds, no matter how coarse a set it may have. It is desirable to utilize the weight of the branch to spread the saw cut; but at the same time the splitting of the wood must be guarded against.

First Method of Removing Limb.—There are two methods of sawing off a limb properly. Plate 28, Fig. 1, shows the tree. Begin with a cut on the under side of the limb, about eight or ten inches from the shoulder, sawing about half way through, Plate 28, Fig. 2. Then remove the saw and make the cut close to the shoulder, as in Plate 28, Fig. 3. When the limb is cut about two-thirds or three-quarters across, the weight of the end will cause it to split up to the under cut, and it will fall off, Plate 28, Fig. 4. You can then safely finish the cut, supporting the stub with the hand, so that none of the bark is stripped.

Second Method of Removing Limb.—In the case of a large limb, as in Plate 29, Fig. 1, the swelling at the base may be such that it will not split horizontally, and then there

PLATE 28.—FIRST METHOD OF REMOVING BRANCH.

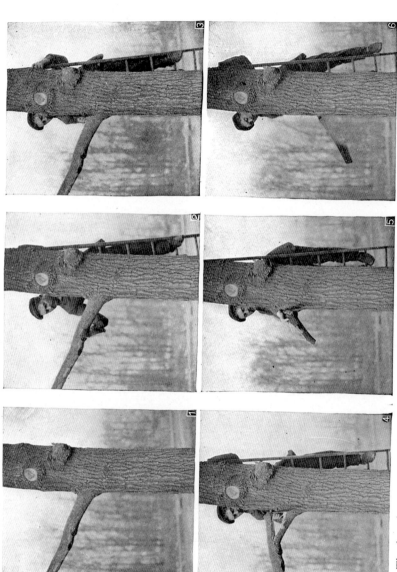

1. The branch. 2. Start with an undercut, saw about half way through. 3. Then saw close to the shoulder. 4. Branch will split horizontally and fall off. 5. Finish cut. 6. Branch is removed.

will be risk of the limb's splitting at the shoulder. In such case begin as before with an undercut, Plate 29, Fig. 2; then, in order to utilize the weight of the end of the limb to spread the cut for the clearance of the saw, cut close to the shoulder, about half way through the limb, Plate 29, Fig. 3. Then remove the saw, and cut on top of the limb, a little above the undercut, Plate 29, Fig. 4. When the two saw-cuts meet on the same level, the limb will drop off, Plate 29, Fig. 4. Then finish as before, by sawing off the stub.

The Rule to Follow.—Hence the rule for the proper removal of a limb is: Always begin with an undercut about eight or ten inches from the base of the limb you want to remove. Then saw close to the shoulder, as has been pointed out before. When past the centre of the limb, proceed cautiously. If the swelling at the base of the limb is not too great, the limb will split horizontally, turn about the remaining stub as a pivot, and fall off. You can then safely finish the cut. If, however, the chances are that the limb will not split horizontally, but break at the shoulder, saw above the undercut till the limb drops off and then remove the stub. By following the above directions there is no danger of causing injury to the trunk of a tree.

Healing of Scar.—The time it takes a pruning-scar to heal completely depends upon its size and the rapidity of growth of the tree. A rapidly growing tree, like the Carolina poplar, can heal a wound on its trunk, three or four inches in diameter, in one growing season; while it takes a hard maple a few years to accomplish a like result. While the callus is overgrowing the scar from the periphery toward the centre, the end grain of the remaining stub is exposed to the weather. The wood dries and checks, and although all precautions may have been taken to remove

PLATE 29.—SECOND METHOD OF REMOVING BRANCH.

1. The branch.   2. Start with an undercut, saw half way.   3. Then saw close to the shoulder, about half way.   4. Saw above undercut, branch will drop off.   5. Remove stub.   6. Work is done.

the limb close to the trunk, by the time the wound heals the decay may be carried deeply into the tree.

A Dressing Must be Applied.—It is necessary, therefore, to apply a dressing to the surface of a scar when a limb is removed that will, as far as possible, prevent the decay of the old wood until it is overcapped with new callus. Thick paint makes a good dressing; but the best way of preserving the condition of the exposed stub is by an application of thick coal-tar.[1] This fills the pores of the wood; and, when it sets, becomes as hard as enamel. It checks the evaporation of the sap and prevents the entrance of water. The coal-tar also acts as an antiseptic, and prevents the formation by moisture and dust of a fertile spot for the entrance of fungus spores and insects.

The function of dressings is not to hasten the growth of the callus; but simply to prevent the decay of the stub. In the case of scars, two or three inches in diameter, on hard-wood trees, one application of coal-tar will be sufficient to keep the exposed wood intact until the healing process is completed. Larger scars may need further applications of tar, one in about every two years, until the surface is overgrown. So long as the exposed wood is kept intact, there is no danger of injury resulting from pruning, no matter how long it takes the wound to heal.

Training to Artificial Forms.—In the city of Paris, street-trees are sometimes trained to artificial geometrical forms.

---

[1] Coal-tar is a waste product of gas works obtained in the process of distilling bituminous coal in retorts. The crude tar contains carbolic acid and other impurities that may corrode plant tissues if present in large quantities. The coal-tar found on the market is usually a refined product from which the injurious ingredients have been removed. The coal-tar sold for roof-coating is an efficient and safe dressing for wounds. One must avoid the use of tars having injurious elements in their composition.

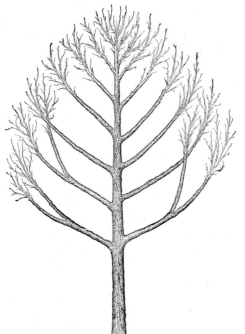

Such formal treatment of trees is a matter of taste; but trees always appear more interesting and exhibit more individual character when their natural mode of growth is preserved as much as possible. In this country the training of trees into unnatural symmetrical shapes is little practised.

FIG. 21.—Oriental Plane, fifty feet in height, denuded at the base; to be headed back.

Keeping Crown Within Limits. —Street-trees, however, should not be permitted to grow beyond certain bounds, for a number of reasons. It is desirable to restrict the spread of trees when they begin to touch houses or extend over the roadway so as to give too much shade. To maintain a compact crown on some trees, it is necessary to shorten the ends

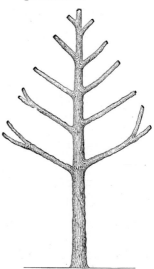

FIG. 22.—The same Oriental Plane, headed back to three-quarters of the original height, with the lateral branches shortened in proportion.

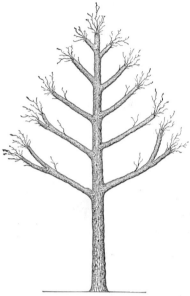

FIG. 23.—The same Oriental Plane a year after the operation.

of the branches to send more energy into the portions near the stem. The diameter of the root system of a tree is about the same as that of the crown. On city streets, where the soil is usually poor and the growth of the roots restricted, the ends of the branches become ragged in time, the foliage thin, and finally the top of the tree dies back,

producing a condition known as "stag-head" or "top-dry." Trees can be maintained in better condition by limiting the spread of the top so as to reduce the draft on the roots, and frequently failing specimens can be restored to vigor by shortening the branches.

Heading Back Old Trees.—When early pru-

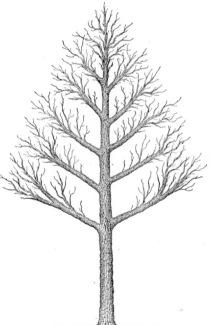

FIG. 24.—The same Oriental Plane several years after the operation.

ning is neglected the problems of restoring trees to symmetry, of suppressing certain branches, and of forcing others become very difficult. Not all trees have the same power of sending out new shoots when branches are cut back. Rapidly growing trees, like planes, soft maples, elms, and poplars, lend themselves more readily to heading back than other trees. One of the advantages of the use of the planes as street-trees is that they recover quickly from the effects of severe pruning.

When trees are cut back, numerous shoots develop from buds near the ends of the remaining branches. Plane-trees especially send out a whorl of new twigs. Two or three years after heading back, it is necessary to suppress or entirely remove some of these new branches, and leave only the more vigorous ones to maintain the growth of the top. Figs. 21 to 24 show the various steps in the process of restoration of an old oriental plane that had become denuded at the base.

An instrument called a dendroscope, Fig. 25, devised by Des Cars,[1] is sometimes helpful when shaping or heading back a number of trees to the same form and dimensions. It consists of a piece of thin paper or wooden board, about 4 x 8 inches, in which is cut an opening proportional in outline to the form it is desired to give the trees. With this device the foreman can indicate to the pruner in the tree the exact places where cuts should be made.

The foreman stands removed from the tree at a distance about equal to its height, holds the dendroscope vertically and at such a distance from the eye that when he looks through the opening, the bottom of it coincides with the base of the tree and the top with the place marking the height to

[1] "A Treatise on Pruning Forest and Ornamental Trees," by A. Des Cars.

which the tree is to be cut back.   As he stands in one position he directs the cutting of all the branches that are parallel
to the plane of the card.   Then he slowly goes round the
tree and indicates where the other branches are to be cut.

Sometimes when large branches are removed close to the
trunk, adventitious or dormant buds near the place where
the cut was made are stimulated into a forced growth,
and they produce suckers or water
sprouts.   If these are desirable to
fill out the crown they should be
retained; but if they occur low on
the trunk they should be removed,
for they rob the upper branches of
food materials.

When to Prune.—Careful attention to the time of pruning shade-
trees is not so important as in
the case of trimming shrubs for
flowers and fruit-trees for fruit.
Very heavy pruning and heading

FIG. 25.—A Dendroscope.

back of old trees are best done in very late fall or during
the winter, when trees are dormant.   The store of reserve
material will cause a rapid growth of new shoots the following spring.

The shaping of trees can be done best when the foliage
is on.   It is also easier to discover dead, imperfect, and
weak branches.   For general pruning, therefore, it may be
said that any time after midsummer is a good time to prune.
During the spring and the early summer, when the sap is
most active, it is apt to flow too freely from the wounds,
and prevent the adhesion of any dressing, and the bark can
be easily stripped from the trunk by accidental splitting of

branches. At this time also the removal of very much of
the crown is apt to react unfavorably upon the roots by
robbing them of so much elaborated food material. It has
not been observed that the rapidity of the healing of the
wounds is dependent to any extent upon the season when
pruning is done.

Pruning Tools.—While the tools required for pruning are
simple, one will find that a great deal of experimenting will
be required to strike the right kind. The saw is the chief
requisite, and the kinds actually sold as pruning-saws are
very inefficient. A cross-cut saw, that is satisfactory for
cutting dry, seasoned wood, is worthless for sawing the
sappy, tough wood which is at the base of a limb, where it
joins the trunk. After a great deal of trials with all kinds
of saws, the writer was on the point of having a special
kind of saw made, when he discovered on the market a saw
which is far more satisfactory than any other commonly
used for pruning. It is Atkins' Universal Saw, No. 83,
having a patent tooth, as shown in Plate 30, Fig. 4, and is admirable for the green wood of living trees. It works easy,
and there is no pressure required on the saw to make it cut.
Work can be done very rapidly with this tool.

The best way to carry the saw when going up a tree is
to suspend it from a belt having a loop provided for that
purpose. When hung just behind the hip it leaves the arms
and body of the pruner free to climb or shin up any
branches. Plate 30, Fig. 8, shows an admirable form of
pruner's belt for carrying a saw, a small axe, a rope, and a
leather holder for supporting the pruner's body while working. The holder is passed around the tree and the ends
clasped to two rings in the belt, one on each side of the
body. When not in use it is suspended from one of the

PLATE 30.—PRUNING TOOLS.

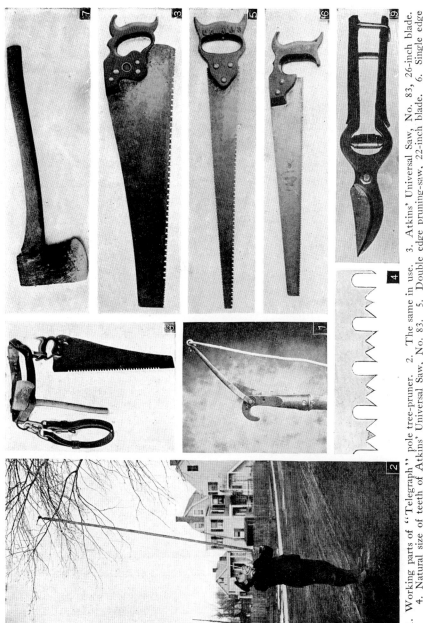

1. Working parts of "Telegraph" pole tree-pruner. 2. The same in use. 3. Atkins' Universal Saw, No. 83, 26-inch blade. 4. Natural size of teeth of Atkins' Universal Saw, No. 83. 5. Double edge pruning-saw, 22-inch blade. 6. Single edge pruning-saw, 20-inch blade. 7. Pruning-axe, weight 2¼ pounds, handled. Length of handle, 18 inches. 8. Pruner's belt, with holder and tools. 9. Hand pruning-shears; length, 9 inches.

rings of the belt. A rope, when necessary, can also be attached to one of the rings.

A small, one-handed axe is used to remove sprouts, suckers, and dead twigs and small branches. A pole-saw is used on the end of long branches. A combination chisel and hook, Fig. 26, on a long pole, can be used to pull down dead limbs at the tops of trees, and also to remove suckers and sprouts. It is operated either by a downward stroke of the hook or an upward one of the chisel. The cutting edge of the chisel is concave, so that it does not glance off to one side when striking a branch.

FIG. 26.—Combination chisel and hook.

To shape the ends of the lower limbs of trees and to remove small twigs up to an inch in diameter, the pole-pruner will be found an extremely efficient tool. Of these tools, there are many on the market; but some of them fall to pieces after a few hours' work. One of the best pole-pruners made is the "Telegraph" tree-pruner shown in Plate 30, Fig. 1. It is best to buy the pruner separately, and have a pole especially made.   This should be of straight grained spruce, two inches in diameter and twelve or fourteen feet long. Plate 30, Fig. 2, shows the method of using it. It is operated by means of a rope, and the spiral spring brings the knife into position again for another cut. Extra knives and springs can be bought, so that they can be easily replaced when broken. The pruner will last through a summer's work in good condition.

Hand pruning-shears are useful for cutting back trees when setting them out, and for pruning broken roots; also in shaping young trees during their first few years of growth. The cutting part of pruning-shears is the one blade—the crescent shaped portion just presses against the branch. When using the shears they should be held in such a way that the crescent is turned toward the side of the branch that is being removed. When trimming back twigs the cuts should be made about half an inch or an inch above a strong bud, which on developing will continue the growth of the branch. The short stub will dry and fall off, so that the active tissue near the bud will form a callus over the wound. When the cut is made too close to the bud, it is likely to be injured by drying, and will not develop.

When removing heavy branches it is sometimes best to support the ends, and a rope and pulley-blocks are found very useful. When cutting back the ends of branches that cannot easily be reached by a ladder, the workmen can support themselves partly by means of ropes attached to the belt, and running over a crotch near the stem at the top of the tree.

Hints to Tree-Climbers.—The Department of Parks of the Boroughs of Brooklyn and Queens issues, in pamphlet form, the following "Hints to Tree-Climbers" to its men:

"1. Before starting out on a tree, judge its general condition. The trunk of a tree that shows age, disease, or wood-destroying insects generally has its branches in an equally unhealthy condition. Greater precautions should, therefore, be taken with a tree in this condition than with a young, vigorous tree.

"2. The different kinds of wood differ naturally in their strength and pliability. The soft and brash woods need greater precautions than the strong and pliable ones. All the poplars, the ailantus, the silver maple, the chestnut,

catalpa, and willow are either too soft or brittle to depend
on without special care.   The elm, hickory, and oak have
strong, flexible woods and are, therefore, safer than any
others.   The red oak is weaker than the other oaks.   The
sycamore and beech have a tough cross-grained wood and
are, therefore, fairly strong.   The linden has a soft wood,
while the ash and gum, though strong and flexible, are apt
to split.

"3. Look out for a limb that shows fungous growths.
Every fungus sends out a lot of fibers into the main body of
the limb which draw out its sap.   The interior of the branch
then loses all strength and becomes like powder.   Outside
appearances sometimes do not show the interior condition,
but one can be sure that every time he sees a fungus prop-
ping out, there is trouble behind it, and the limb is not alto-
gether safe.

"4. When a limb is full of holes or knots, it generally
indicates that borers have been working all kinds of galleries through it, making it unsafe.   The silver maple and
sycamore maple are especially full of borers, which in many
cases work on the under side of the branch, so that the man
in the tree looking down cannot see its dangerous condition.

"5. A dead limb with bark falling off indicates that it
died at least three months before and is, therefore, less safe
than one with its bark tightly adhering to it.

"6. Branches are more apt to snap on a frosty day when
they are covered with an icy coating than on a warm, summer day.

"7. A rainy or drizzly day causes the branches of a tree
to be slippery, and greater precautions are then necessary.

"8. Always use the pole-saw and pole-shear on the tips

of long branches, and use the pole-hook in removing dead branches of the ailantus and other brittle trees where it would be too dangerous to reach them otherwise.

"9. Examine your ladder before using it.

"10. Be sure of the strength of your branch before tying an extension-ladder to it.

"11. Do not slant the extension-ladder too much.

"12. Always watch the upper end of your ladder.

"13. Do not forget to use the 'danger sign' on streets where falling branches are apt to injure careless passers-by.

"14. Always consult your foreman before taking up any job where risk is involved."

CHAPTER VII

INJURIES TO SHADE-TREES AND HOW TO
PROTECT THEM

EVEN in the forest the enemies of trees are very many. Winds break their limbs, snow and ice maim and deform them, hail beats off their leaves and twigs, frost nips their buds and tender shoots, lightning shatters them, and fungi and insects prey upon them. Added to natural enemies, the unfavorable city conditions make the life of a street-tree a hard one.

The intelligent planting of trees must be supplemented by their protection, both by personal and legal means. It is idle to plant trees unless their safety can be assured. The vast majority of people have no conception that a tree has any right to be respected, just as they are slow of comprehension where the rights of animals are in question, or the right of posterity to what we now enjoy.

There is another point to be remembered in dealing with trees; that while they are living objects, and in their modes of growth and reproduction greatly resemble animals, they do not possess the power of locomotion. If a man dislikes his environment, he moves to a more congenial place. A tree cannot move, and its surroundings must be made agreeable to its well being. The writer has often thought of what would happen if trees could run away from the place where they are maltreated and abused. Many people would

136

find their specimens gone—departed to more hospitable regions.

The chief sources of injury to street-trees are:

POOR SOIL

The street-soil is generally very poor and the trees constantly take the available plant-food out of it. A part of this matter assimilated by the trees is converted into wood; but by far the larger portion goes into the leaves. In the forest the fallen leaves pile up and form a humus, by means of which the mineral matter contained in the leaves is returned to the soil. In the city, however, the successive crops of leaves are removed and the soil becomes impoverished. Just as one would not think of success in farming without the yearly use of fertilizers of some sort to enrich the ground, so in the case of shade-trees, the periodic application of some suitable fertilizer to the soil about them is of the highest importance to aid their growth.

ROOTS LACK AIR AND WATER

To insure the proper performance of the tree's functions its roots must have a supply of air and water. The exclusion of either of these requisites from the soil is fatal. It is a matter of common observation that a filling of earth, two or three feet deep, about a thrifty tree will damage or kill it. The covering of earth works this injury simply by excluding air from the active rootlets. Street-trees are greatly limited in their supply of air and moisture by the pavements.

SALT WATER

Salt used in freezing ice-cream is sometimes emptied near trees. When it is dissolved by rains and carried to the roots it becomes very injurious. Plate 33, Fig. 6.

DUST, SMOKE, AND INJURIOUS GASES IN THE AIR

Dust and smoke are liable to choke up the breathing pores of the leaves, and their natural functions are severely hindered. Some trees suffer more than others from this nuisance. The leaves of the sugar maple are especially susceptible; their stomata or breathing pores become clogged up by dust, and they acquire a hard, metallic state.

In cities where large quantities of bituminous coal are used and in the vicinity of manufacturing establishments, such as fertilizer mills, paper-pulp mills, copper-smelting and blast furnaces, particularly where sulfur gases are produced, the effects upon all kinds of foliage are very evident. It has been shown that sulfuric-acid gas is the most injurious component of the fumes that prove injurious to foliage, and European investigations have proved that the presence of sulfuric-acid gas in the air, in the ratio of 1 to 50,000, is enough to lead to the destruction of the leaves of deciduous trees. The effects of sulfurous fumes are shown by the turning of the leaves reddish-brown in spots or along the edges, and eventually of their drying up entirely.

All the evidence goes to show that little can be done toward mitigating the trouble caused by poisonous gases in the air. In cities suffering from the smoke nuisance it is very difficult to grow many of the ordinary street-trees. The European and the American planes will stand adverse conditions better than any of the other good street-trees.

OILING OF ROADS

The oiling of roadways during the last few years has led to a great deal of speculation regarding the effect of the dust from such roads on the vegetation bordering them. No case of injury to the foliage of trees or shrubs resulting from the oiling of roads has come to the observation of the writer. The Director of Public Roads of the United States Department of Agriculture writes, under date of September 2, 1910: "I am pleased to advise that from personal observations and from conversations with officials in a position to know, I am confident that where roads are oiled, so that the roots of trees or shrubbery do not come in contact with the oil, no injury occurs to the foliage."

On the other hand, the writer noticed some items in the newspapers stating that in Paris the oiling of streets proved injurious to foliage. He wrote to the Prefect of the Seine, who has charge of the street-trees of Paris, and under date of August 23, 1910, received, through the American Ambassador in Paris, a reply as follows:

"I am just in receipt of a report of the Commissioner of the Western Section of Thoroughfares, in which the latter indicates the baneful effect of the spreading of hot tar upon the Avenue du Bois de Boulogne, and proposes to call the attention of the Public Roads Service to the withering of the trees on the avenue which, in his opinion, must be attributed to the tarring of this road.

"It appears from this report that a border-plot of stonecrops was burned in 1908, and lost its leaves the very day after the spreading; that some geraniums, and some begonias showed leaves shriveled, spotted, and their growth stopped. It was the same with some lilac, currant, and gooseberry bushes.

"This year, likewise, many of the trees on the Avenue du Bois are in an alarming state of decay; several specimens of ailantus, maple, and American walnut, formerly in good vegetation, are dead. Others are in a drooping state.

"The Commissioner of the Western Section believes that this condition arises from the deposit, upon the leaves, of the tar-dust stirred up by the intense circulation of vehicles.

"The Public Roads Service will be informed of these facts; and perhaps it will be necessary to decide to abandon the tarring in the proximity of vegetation."

While the above letter would seem to indicate that there is a relation of cause and effect between the tarring of the Bois de Boulogne and the damage to near-by trees the case is not to be regarded as fully proved. The assigning of the cause of the wilting of the foliage does not seem to be conclusive. The statement about the dying of the stone-crops the very next day after the tar was applied to the road, would lead one to suspect that possibly fumes from the tar were responsible for the injury rather than tar-dust, for a fresh application of oil or tar effectively lays the dust.

The subject needs further very careful study before any definite conclusions can be drawn. The writer has begun some experiments to determine the effect of dust collected from oiled roads on the foliage of trees; but has not yet reached any satisfactory results.

ILLUMINATING GAS

This is extremely poisonous, and is fatal to any tree the roots of which are exposed to it for a sufficient length of time. It is one of the hardships to which city-trees are exposed that it is not always easy to prevent or foresee. Frequently trees are killed before the leak is discovered.

While poor construction of mains is frequently responsible for gas-leaks, breaks in mains occur from a great many causes. Trolley-cars, steam-rollers, and other heavy traffic on highways sometimes cause loosening of joints and even

PLATE 51.—INJURIES BY GAS AND OVERHEAD WIRES.

1. First symptoms of gas-poisoning, partial defoliation. 2. Testing for leaking gas-main by driving down crowbar. The red maple in this case shows a case of severe poisoning. All the leaves are shriveled up. 3. Trees killed by gas. Gas company repairing mains. 4. Trunk of Sugar Maple, about six weeks after having been killed by gas. The bark has begun to shed. The fungus on the trunk is a sap-rot *Hopaloptius gilvus*. 5. White Elms on Jerome Avenue, New York, ruined beyond repair by overhead wires.

breaking of gas-pipes, and the resulting leaks sometimes kill a row of trees of an entire block.

A very small leak does not saturate the soil at once, and may not be the cause of the immediate death of a tree. Its effect is bound to tell in time, however. The tree will assume an unhealthy look, the foliage will become yellow and thin at the top and there will appear a large amount of dead wood that will not be accounted for in any other way.

Symptoms of Gas-Poisoning.—The symptoms of gas-poisoning are characteristic. The effect of a large leak upon a tree is very pronounced. The foliage turns yellow, wilts, and falls from the tree. There is no mistaking the cause. The effect of a small leak is yellowing of the foliage, followed by a greater or less defoliation of the tree, according to the degree of poisoning. Limbs here and there die, the bark becomes loosened in places, and fungous growths make their appearance on the trunk and the main branches. The poisoned soil generally becomes darker than its natural color. The roots and the sapwood of the lower trunk become discolored blue, and have a most offensive odor.

The writer recalls a case when he very carefully watched a number of street-trees affected by gas-poisoning. There were several varieties among them. The elms died first, and soon afterward the bark began to loosen and drop from the trunk and main branches. The sugar maples died next. The red maples withstood the effects of the gas the longest. One red maple in particular was observed for about three weeks, the ground at the roots of which was badly saturated with gas. The foliage did not dry up at once, but gradually dropped from the tree, beginning at the top. Ulcers were formed on the trunk and main branches, and the sap oozed out from splits in the bark. It was frothy white and had a fermented odor, as that of cider. Finally, all the foliage of the tree was gone, the sap stopped flowing, and the tree was dead.

The formation of ulcers and the oozing of sap are not necessary symptoms of gas-poisoning, however, but may follow other diseased or weakened conditions of trees. See page 199.

The wilting of the foliage of a tree following its attack by borers is sometimes mistaken for gas-poisoning. When a branch of a tree becomes riddled, the exposed wood dries and checks, and in the course of time the draft of sap is interrupted and the end of the branch dies. The wilting of the foliage in such cases makes one suspicious of gas. An examination of the branch, however, will reveal the true source of injury.

How to Detect Leaks.—The presence of gas can be detected by making a hole in the ground, three or four feet deep, with a crowbar, and applying the nostrils to the opening. Unless the leak is extremely slight, the gas can usually be discovered by the above method. A more certain way of proceeding, however, is to insert a piece of gas or other pipe into the hole made by the crowbar, and draw up and inhale through the nostrils or the mouth the gases at the base of the opening. The slightest amount of gas in the soil can be detected in this way. When the gas is present in the soil in large quantities, it can be ignited by applying a match at the opening made with a crowbar. It will burn with a flash. This method, however, should not be used in testing for gas-leaks. It is extremely dangerous, as it is likely to result in an explosion of the gas-main.

When a slight leak is discovered before the injury proceeds very far, the tree can be saved by quickly repairing

the leak and aerating the soil.   This can be done by leaving
the ditch open, digging a channel around the tree, loosening
the soil about the roots, and watering freely.

Laying of Gas-Mains.—Care in laying gas-mains is of the
utmost importance.   The leaking of gas is a great loss to
the gas companies, and economizing the cost of first con-

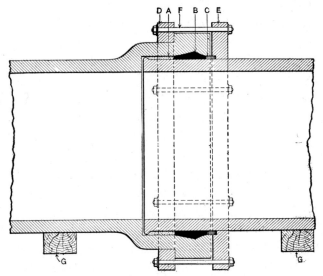

FIG, 27.—Method of making tight joints in gas-pipes. A, Untarred oakum or
hemp.   B, Calked lead.   C, Rubber packing.   D and E, Two malleable
iron sectional rings.   F, Bolts for drawing the rings together so as to press
down rubber packing C.   G, G, Wooden blocks for supporting ends of pipes.

struction is likely to prove disastrous in the long run.
Sometimes gas-pipes are laid with cement joints, as this
method is cheap; but the least settling of the ground causes
leaks.   Threaded joints are efficient on small pipes.   One of
the best methods now in use of making tight joints in gas-
pipes, eight inches or more in diameter, is shown in Fig. 27.
Untarred oakum or hemp-yarn is well rammed in first; and
above that is poured melted lead, which is afterward com-

pacted by a calking hammer. Rubber packing is then inserted into the annular space left after the calking of the lead, and rammed into the joint and held there by means of two malleable iron rings connected by bolts. The pipes are supported near the joints by means of blocks of wood to prevent settling.

Damages for Trees Killed.—The injury to trees from gas has been so conclusively demonstrated, and damages have been so frequently awarded for loss of trees by this means in several States, that companies usually settle with property-owners out of court.

In the State of Massachusetts there are a number of cases on record of payments made by gas companies for killing trees by gas. In 1905, the trees along Middlesex Street, Lowell, began to die. Owners obtained investigation by the Park Commission, and the cause was found to be a leaking gas-main. A complaint against the Lowell Gaslight Company was made by the superintendent of parks, and tried in the police court. The company was fined $900, which was paid to the city, and settlements were made with most of the owners.

In 1907, several cases were entered against the Springfield Gaslight Company, but they were all settled out of court. In one case twenty-eight trees on one street were damaged by gas, and the company paid the owners an aggregate sum of a little over $2,000, as agreed by a committee.

In the majority of cases, however, no amount of money can restore the loss of large trees. Continued vigilance is necessary on the part of property-owners and city tree officials to prevent trees from being killed. When there is the slightest suspicion of a gas-leak, tests of the soil should be made. The trees along streets having large gas-mains need especial watching. The soil around the roots should be tested at frequent intervals, and repairs of mains immediately ordered if the presence of gas is detected.

Tests for gas should be made in the spring, as soon as the frost is out of the ground. During the winter the frozen surface causes an accumulation of gas underneath when there is the slightest leak. When gas is discovered at that season of the year and the leak stopped, there is a chance for the affected tree to recover. On the other hand, if the gas is left in the soil it will poison the tree when it resumes active growth.

OVERHEAD WIRES

The injury to trees from overhead wires is frequently serious. While cases of wanton destruction of roadside-trees, to make way for telephone, telegraph, electric-light, and trolley-wires, have been numerous in the past, greater vigilance on the part of property-owners and public officials has caused a lessening of the evil. There may still be found, however, hundreds of trees in public highways that have been lopped, butchered, hacked out of their former shapeliness by ruthless linemen, who regard nothing with greater contempt than a tree. These crippled shapes are painful to look upon, as are all misshapen or mutilated things, and the pity of it is that a little precaution, a trifle clemency, might have left the greater number of them uninjured.

The laying of wires underground is becoming more common. In many cities ordinances have been enacted requiring public utility companies to put their wires underground at the rate of a number of miles each year, and no new lines are permitted to be constructed above ground. So long, however, as there are overhead telephone, electric-light, and trolley-feed wires in cities, there will be interference with trees, and it will require continuous watchfulness to reduce the evil to a minimum.

In the first place, it should not be permitted to attach wires of any kind to trees on a public highway. Sometimes, as in the case of the telephone, it is not the wire that does the mischief, but the way it is attached to the tree. If rope is used, it does not harm the tree. If wire is employed instead, and is allowed to remain on the tree for a number of years, it girdles the limb and kills it. Such cases are very numerous. The wire is not noticed, and it is only when a dead branch appears on the tree that the fatal wire is discovered. Sometimes when the central stem of a tree is so girdled, the entire top dies and the tree is ruined. Then, again, linemen, unless especially cautioned, use metal spurs to climb trees, and great injury is likely to result to the tree from such a practise. Sometimes a man's foot slips and a deep gash is inflicted on the limb.

Escaping Electrical Currents.—Where wires pass through trees, they should not be allowed to come in contact with limbs, because their swaying causes an abrasion of the bark. The continuous rubbing prevents the healing of the wound; in time the wood dries and checks, the limb decays, and breaks in a storm. In fact, it has been found that all the ill effects of wires running through trees are the result of mechanical injuries followed by decay. The instances of direct killing of trees because of escaping electricity are very rare. It is during wet weather, when live wires touch a tree, that there is a grounding of the electric current through it. Frequently local damage results by the burning of the part in contact with the wire or cable.

How to Protect Branches.—A limb may be effectively protected from abrasion by an electric light or trolley-feed wire in contact with it by a strip of wood fastened to it by means of two nails, one at each end. The strip should not be nailed against the limb, but should be separated from it by two pieces of insulating fiber, half an inch thick, as shown in Fig. 28.

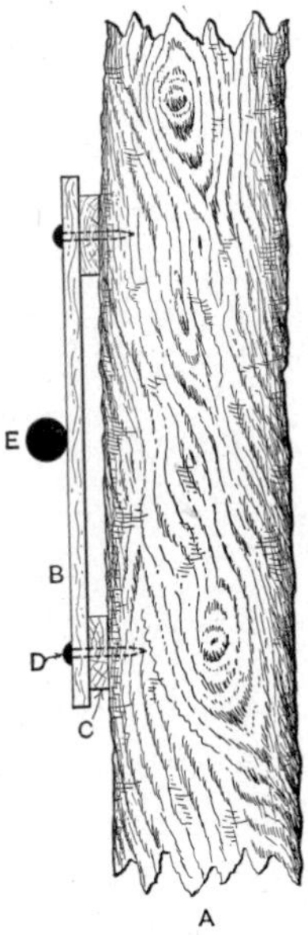

In no case should the cutting of limbs of shade-trees for the purpose of making way for wires be permitted; but should an exceptional case arise, where cutting of limbs is necessary, the work should be done under the supervision of some city official.

There is one case of the evil of overhead wires that cannot be overcome except by their removal, and that is where young trees grow under a web of wires. The young shoots cannot force themselves between the wires, but become stunted, and the result is an abnormally shaped, flat-headed tree. The most horrible butchery occurs when a large, wedge-shaped space is taken out of the centre of beautiful trees to allow the passage of wires. The damage is beyond repair, and it would be better to cut the trees down entirely than to leave permanent eyesores. See Plate 31, Fig. 5.

FIG. 28.—Method of protecting a branch from abrasion by wire cable. A, Branch. B, Strip of wood about 12 inches long, 2½ inches wide. C, Piece of insulating fiber, 2 inches square, ½ inch thick. D, Nail. E, Section of cable.

Damages for Injuries.—Many cases are on record in which damages have been awarded by courts for injury to

trees.   The case of Dr. John Marshall against the American
Telegraph and Telephone Company, tried in the Pennsylvania courts, was an important one.   During the absence of
Dr. John Marshall from his farm at Douglassville, Berks
County, Pa., in 1895, employees of the American Telegraph
and Telephone Company cut down sixty-eight trees on his
property; whereupon Dr. Marshall immediately brought
criminal action against these employees, which action was
carried from the court of the Justice of the Peace to the
Common Pleas Court in Reading, Berks County, and thence
to the Superior Court, with decisions against the telephone
company throughout the entire action.

The fines required of the three employees of the company were to the full limit of the law, and aggregated $150.
The criminal suit having been decided by the highest court
in favor of Dr. Marshall, he brought civil action against the
company for damages, and on January 3, 1898, the court
appointed three viewers to assess damages.   On February
14, 1898, the viewers filed their report, from which report
the telephone company and also Dr. Marshall appealed, and
on October 18, 1898, the case was tried before the Common
Pleas Court in Berks County.   The verdict was in favor
of Dr. Marshall.   The telephone company appealed to the
superior court, and on April 16, 1901, an opinion in favor of
Dr. Marshall was handed down by Justice Beaver, allowing
damages to the amount of $400 to Dr. Marshall.

In his decision, Justice Beaver said in part: "The commercial idea that the only good tree is a dead tree—that is,
that it is only good for lumber—no longer prevails.   The
tree has much more than a commercial value.   Its influence
upon climate and water-supply has come to be regarded as a
question to be reckoned with in determining the conditions

under which our increasingly dense population is to live and flourish. Its beauty and sightliness have value in the landscape. Its shade refreshes and shelters; and even as an investment, young trees have an actual money value which cannot be disregarded or measured by their present value as timber trees."

Another decision of far-reaching importance to telephone and telegraph companies and other companies maintaining lines of poles and wires in public highways, and to owners of property along such highways, was rendered November 17, 1904, by Supreme Court Justice Garretson, in Long Island City.

It was the case of Mary I. Weeks, a resident of Bayside, Long Island, against the New York and New Jersey Telephone Company. The company erected a line of telephone poles on a *public highway* running through her property, and strung wires thereon. The justice held that the use of the highway for the support of a line of poles and wires for supplying the general public with electricity was in no sense a *proper street use*, and that therefore, notwithstanding the statute and the city permits, the erection and maintenance of that line of poles and wires for that purpose without Mrs. Weeks's consent, was unauthorized and illegal. He directed the sheriff to remove its poles and wires from the street.

STREET IMPROVEMENTS

Many trees necessarily fall a sacrifice to important improvements in the natural growth of cities. When large buildings are erected on business streets, close to the sidewalk, it is inevitable that they must go. Trees also suffer from the mutilation of the needed cutting of large roots in resetting curbstones and flag walks; also in the digging for

PLATE 32.—INJURIES TO STREET-TREES.

1. Leader of a 14-inch buckeye broken as a result of abrasion by trolley feed-wire. 2. Top of a 22-inch Sugar Maple, killed by girdling telephone wire. 3. Where the provision for street-trees has been a matter of little concern. 4. Planting strip absent and pavement close to trunk. 5. Sidewalk too narrow; trees planted in gutter in consequence. 6. Trees saved in Cambridge, Mass. Trees planted before street improvement, allowed to project into gutter; curb being interrupted.

water and gas mains and sewers. Such cases arise from time to time in municipal work, but it is highly important that contractors and builders should consult the proper city officials when it is proposed to do any work that is likely to injure trees. Frequently a way is found of accomplishing the results sought without injuring a tree. In many instances a tree may be saved when it seems inevitable to some that it should be sacrificed.

The writer recalls a case of two years ago when an architect came to the office of the Shade-Tree Commission, and wanted permission to remove a fourteen-inch sugar maple that stood in the way of a proposed driveway of a house then under construction. He said that he had studied the problem carefully, and that there was no way of constructing the driveway without removing the tree. The premises were examined, and it was found that the tree encroached less than three feet on the line of the proposed roadway; but that by making it slightly curved, it would be an easy matter to keep clear of the tree. The architect did not approve of the plan. Finally he was told that permission would not be granted to remove that tree under the circumstances. He made the driveway curved, and now the owner of the house is very glad that the tree was saved.

Opening New Streets.—Great injury results to trees when new streets are opened or the grade of streets is changed. In such cases city engineers and boards of public improvement are frequently as great offenders as public utilities companies. Engineers dislike to deviate from straight lines in the laying of streets, or to change the width of a street, even if by so doing it is possible to save a line of trees. When a street department works in conjunction with that in charge of the care of trees, it is sometimes possible to devise means by which trees may be saved. The writer remembers a street in East Orange that was to be macadamized and curbed. As proposed, the street was to have a thirty-foot roadway. To have carried out that plan would have necessitated the cutting down of five red maples, about twenty inches in diameter. On consultation

FIG. 29.—A "well" constructed about an elm-tree when grade was raised.

with the Shade-Tree Commission, the city engineer finally decided to make the roadway twenty-six feet in width, and the trees were permitted to remain.

Changing Grade.—When the street grade is raised or lowered, and there are trees along the line, a problem again arises as to the disposition of the trees. A good deal depends upon the condition of the existing trees. If the grade of a street is lowered about a foot, the trees can safely remain. When the grade is lowered considerably, and the trees are less than a foot in diameter, it will pay to lower them. Very frequently an entire row of trees can be saved that way. If the trees are in poor condition, however, it is best to cut them down and plant new ones. With proper selection, planting, and care, better trees result in a short time than if an attempt is made to save poor specimens.

When the grade of a street is raised, the filling should not be brought up close to the tree, as the exclusion of air will kill it. A well should be left around the tree of as large a diameter as possible. In a few years the roots will come to the surface, and then it will be possible to fill the well and bring the soil up to grade. A grating may be placed over the opening to the well so as to guard against any one's falling into it.

When the street-grade is raised it is even possible to continue the concrete pavement close to the tree, provided an air-space is left underneath that covers as large an extent of root spread as possible. The pavement should not touch the trunk of the tree, but should keep clear of it, six inches or more to allow for the growth of the tree and the circulation of air.

In the New York Zoological Garden, many animal cages having concrete floors were built around large trees, twenty inches and more in diameter. All the trees were saved by raising the floor a foot or more above the ground and leaving an air-space between them. The tree-trunks were allowed to pass through circular openings in the floor, and were protected by means of iron guards so that the animals could not injure them. The work was done under the direction of Hermann W. Merkel, the Forester of the Garden.

Many cases arise in a city, involving the care and preservation of valuable trees. Each case should be studied carefully, and the best plan followed. In cities having shade-tree departments, the people always have the sense of security that the safety of their trees is being guarded; and, if any are to be sacrificed, it is because of inevitable conditions. If, after careful consideration, it is found that there must be cutting of limbs or roots of trees, the work should be done under the supervision of one in charge of the care of trees.

BUILDING OPERATIONS

There are minor improvements in city streets during which trees are killed or damaged without any show of reason. Guy-ropes are frequently attached to trees in the process of building which bruise or cut them severely. The piling of lumber, bricks, and other material, and careless carting, cause serious injury to trees while construction is under way. In the erection or repair of a building the owner or contractor should put such guards around the neighboring trees as will effectively prevent their being injured.

MUTILATION BY HORSES

Of all mechanical injuries to street-trees, however, none are more numerous nor more fatal than the mutilations caused by horses. One would not have to go very far in any town to find scores of examples of trees as badly mutilated as the one shown in Plate 33, Fig. 3. Such trees owe their present condition to horses that feasted on their bark many years ago. Most cities have ordinances forbidding drivers to tie animals to trees, or to leave them standing near a tree. Occasionally a man is arrested and fined for having allowed his horse to injure a tree, but it is not always an easy matter to catch and punish the offender. Besides, in

PLATE 33.—INJURIES TO STREET-TREES.

1. Large trees on Munn Avenue, East Orange, saved when street was improved by deflecting the sidewalk and leaving the trees above grade.
2. Where a tree is being used for purposes other than ornament and shade. 3. Result of injuries to trees by horses when left unprotected by guards. 4. Damage caused by a guard left around a tree after the tree had become too large for it. 5. Tree killed by binding tree-guard (guard was chipped apart before view was taken). 6. Oriental Plane, near an ice-cream factory, injured by salt water from freezers.

many cases, no fine will compensate for the damage done, because in a few minutes a horse may destroy a tree worth hundreds of dollars, and which no amount of money can replace.

Trees Must Have Guards.—In spite of the greatest care, horses will sometimes bite trees; and the only way to make it impossible for them to do so, is to place guards around all trees. On our public streets no tree is safe from the day of planting until the time of maturity. I have seen trees completely ruined a few hours after they were set out, by the horse of the grocer or butcher, who stopped to make some deliveries. The only thing left to do was to set out new ones in their place. When a larger tree, six or eight inches in diameter, is barked, it cannot be so readily replaced. It is left to grow in its injured state. In case the strip of bark removed by the horse is small, the resulting wound may heal, if a box is placed around the tree to protect it from further injury. When a tree is badly bitten or is exposed to successive mutilations, the bark of the growing tree never covers up the scar so made, and the tree becomes irreparable.

As the tree grows, successive annual layers of wood are added, and its diameter is increased. The portion of the tree that has been stripped of bark does not receive this new growth; but the wood is deposited in a thick roll around the edge of the wound. The exposed wood dries, checks, moisture causes it to rot and form a fertile field for fungus growth and the entrance of borers. After a while the decay is carried to the heart of the tree, and sooner or later it dies. The first cause of the decay and death of many of the trees annually removed from public streets may be traced to the mutilation of the trunks by horses.

Trees with the bark removed are unsightly, and as long as they continue their growth their deformity increases. After a time they also become a source of danger. The weakest part of the trunk of a tree is at a point four or five feet from the ground. It is the portion of the tree that withstands the greatest strain during a storm. For example, if you grasp the end of a rod with the hands and bend it sufficiently, it will break in the middle. The resistance of the roots of a tree, on the one hand, and the pressure of the wind against the head, on the other, produce a like result; the tree tends to break across the trunk. Sometimes during storms mutilated trees snap at the points of the trunks where they had been injured, and cause considerable damage by their fall.

When a tree is supplied with a guard, it must not be allowed to remain after the tree outgrows it. The injury caused by the failure to remove a guard after it becomes too small, is sometimes more fatal than to expose the tree to mutilation. If the guard binding a tree is weak, it yields and breaks; but before giving way under the strain of the tree's growth, it usually injures the trunk. In Plate 33, Fig. 4, is shown the damage caused by a guard left around a tree after the latter had become too large for it. The guard broke; but the tree was disfigured by an abnormal growth of a ring of tissue. If the guard is very strong and the increase of the diameter of the tree continues, the action of the iron band around it has the effect of girdling, and the tree dies. In Plate 33, Fig. 5, is shown an example cf a tree, the death of which was caused by the binding of the protector, which was cut apart before the photograph was taken. The effect of its pressure on the trunk is clearly shown.

CHAPTER VIII

INJURIOUS INSECTS, FUNGOUS AND OTHER DISEASES

BESIDES being subject to injuries resulting from conditions of artificial city environment and abuse, as just described, trees have natural parasitic enemies such as insects and fungi, and also suffer from diseases in which the conditions of soil and climate are the controlling factors.

TREATMENT OF TREES FOR INSECT PESTS

The most vital task, by far, in the care of trees is the extermination of the insects that threaten to destroy or injure them from time to time. The great damage inflicted by insects on shade-trees throughout the country is usually underestimated. A fully grown shade-tree is a valuable asset to any property, and while it is not always possible to estimate its loss in financial terms it must be remembered that it may have taken a lifetime to grow. The value of street-trees is infinitely greater than their cost of planting. They are treasures which should be most jealously guarded. To give an idea of the extensive damage caused by insects attention need be called only to the depradations of the elm-leaf beetle. From 1898 to 1905 it caused the death of several thousand trees in Albany and Troy alone, besides seriously weakening many others. The leopard moth is a very serious borer, which has become established about New York

159

City and has killed hundreds of trees. In the northern section of the State of New Jersey, a great many of the sugar maples died in 1905 and 1906 as a result of the injuries inflicted on these trees by the sugar-maple borer and the leopard moth a few years before that time. The gipsy moth, perhaps the most destructive of all tree-pests, has become firmly established in Massachusetts.

Even in the forest the annual loss of trees from insect pests is very great; but in cities the unfavorable conditions to tree growth are contributory causes that make them still more vulnerable to attack. Like animals, trees can resist disease to a greater degree when they are in a healthy condition. Many insects do not attack trees until they show signs of weakness, and that is especially true of borers. Generally, then, it may be said that one of the best methods of preventing insect injury is to keep trees in as thrifty a condition as possible. It should always be remembered that trees have life—different in kind, perhaps, from that of animals, but nevertheless a life that needs nourishment and favorable conditions for the maintenance of vigor.

While protective measures are extremely important, there will be visitations of diseases and pests that will require remedial treatment. Besides, insects are dependent during their development on plant food, certain species preferring certain trees, so that from a natural standpoint the insect possesses its right to exist just as other forms of life. It is admitted, however, that this point of view is not consoling to one whose trees have been killed by caterpillars, borers, or other pests. It should be recognized as absolutely imperative for the owner of one tree or a thousand trees to be prepared to combat insects when a visitation occurs.

Insects feeding on trees are always present; but sometimes in greater numbers than others. Frequently when a certain species becomes very numerous, natural enemies and parasites develop that kill the greater part or an entire brood. Sometimes during the metamorphosis of insects, unfavorable climatic conditions arise that kill a great number. Again, an insect species may become so numerous as to exhaust the food plant and then the race dies. It should not be permitted, however, to adopt such heroic measures in insect fighting.

The transformations which insects undergo from the time of their hatching from the egg to their maturity is called their metamorphosis. The egg is the first stage in the existence of any insect. Almost always the eggs are laid by the mother insect on or near the plant food which gives nourishment to the young. The larva is the second stage of an insect's life and is the form that hatches from the egg. Familiar examples of larvæ are caterpillars, maggots, and grubs. The larval stage is the feeding period in the life history of most insects injuring shade-trees, and is of supreme importance from an economic standpoint, for it is during this condition that many insects commit their greatest depredations.

The third stage in the life of an insect is the change of the larva into a pupa. Many larvæ, especially those of moths when fully grown, spin about their body silken cases called cocoons, at the same time transforming themselves into pupæ. The pupa remains inactive in the cocoon for some time, then breaks through the cocoon and emerges as the adult or mature insect. Some insects pass the winter or hibernating condition in the egg form, others as partly grown larvæ. Again, many hibernate in the pupal stage and still others pass the winter in the adult condition. The transformation of insects is of interest not only to the nature student but also to one who seeks some method of controlling them. There is always some one of the stages in the insect's metamorphosis when it is most vulnerable and most easily exterminated. It may be the egg, larval, pupal, or adult condition. It is not usually the time when the most injury to trees is apparent. In insect fighting the point constantly to be borne in mind is, as far as possible, to destroy the pests before they develop and reach their most injurious stage. To do that successfully, a knowledge of the life histories of the common tree-pests is absolutely necessary.

Most States publish bulletins descriptive of the common insect pests of shade and ornamental trees, with directions how to combat them. The state entomologists are always at the service of any citizen and are glad to give information in the matter of insect control. It is therefore thought sufficient in this work to describe only the most common and destructive of our shade-tree pests and point out the easiest means of destroying them.

There are three classes of tree-destroying insects which may be grouped as leaf-eating insects, sucking insects, and borers.

LEAF-EATING INSECTS

Leaf-eating insects inflict injury by feeding on the leaf tissue of plants. They can usually be reached by poisoning the leasus with an application of arsenic in some form.

Tussock Moth (*Orgyia leucostigma* S. and A.).—This insect passes the winter in the egg state. The eggs are deposited by the females in September and October in conspicuous white masses on the bark of the trees. About the end of May the larvæ begin to hatch. They immediately take to the leaves, increase in size and go through five

PLATE 34.—LIFE HISTORY OF TUSSOCK MOTH.

1. Egg Masses on bark of White Maple, adult female at A, ovipositing (about ¾ natural size). 2. Larvæ feeding on leaves of American Linden (about ½ natural size). 3. A, Female pupa. B, Male pupa. C, Male pupa. B, Adult male (about ¾ natural size). 4. Horse-chestnut completely defoliated by larvæ.

molts. When they complete their feeding period, nothing but the principal veins of the leaves are left.

The larval period lasts about four or five weeks. Then the caterpillars return to the bark, spin cocoons and change to pupæ. They remain in that condition for two weeks and then emerge as adults. The males are winged and the females wingless. Pairing now takes place, the males die and the females deposit a cluster of eggs for the second brood. Generally from three hundred to five hundred eggs are found in a single cluster, from which if conditions are favorable, as many caterpillars may hatch.

The summer, however, is but half over. Toward the end of July, and the beginning of August, the eggs deposited by the first brood hatch and the young larvæ go up on the leaves to finish the work begun by the parents. The cycle continues as before—through the larval, pupal, and the adult condition. In September the eggs are deposited on the bark of the trees, remain in that condition through the winter, and hatch in the spring.

The easiest and most effective means to control this insect is to exterminate it while it is in its egg condition. The clusters are loosely attached to the bark, are very conspicuous, and are mostly on the trunks and lower limbs. They can be removed either by hand or by scraping them off. After collecting, the egg masses should be burned.

If the eggs are allowed to hatch, the only treatment then possible is to spray the foliage of the tree with a solution of arsenate of lead. (See Insecticides, Chap. IX.) The method of spraying is not always so thorough as removing the egg clusters.

During the last four years, very little spraying has been done in East Orange to control the tussock moth. In spite

PLATE 35.—BROWN TAIL MOTH AND GIPSY MOTH.

1. Life History of Brown Tail Moth (about ⅔ natural size). A, Egg mass. B, Larva. C, Wintering quarters. D, Male pupa. E, Female pupa. H, Cocoons. F, Adult male. G, Adult female. 2. Life History of Gipsy Moth (about ⅔ natural size). G, Egg mass. A, Larva. D, Cocoon. B, Male pupa. C, Female pupa. E, Adult male. F, Adult female.

of the insect's being epidemic in neighboring cities, the trees of East Orange have been kept free from this pest by the collection of the egg masses. This insect usually attacks the elms, the lindens, the white maple, and the horse-chestnut.

Gipsy Moth (*Porthetria dispar* Linn.).—Closely related to the tussock moth in its mode of development, but more destructive of plant life than any other species of pest is the gipsy moth. Its caterpillars thrive on an exceedingly large number of plants. They eat without hesitation almost all of our native trees and shrubs. It is a European insect, which was introduced into the United States in 1869, by a naturalist who imported it in the course of some experiments on silkworms.

The winter is passed in the egg condition. The egg masses are rounded or oval clusters covered with yellowish hair from the body of the female, giving them the appearance of a small piece of sponge. They hatch during May or early June. As a rule the caterpillars feed at night and hide during the day.

When ready to change to pupæ the caterpillars are apt to wander from their food, sometimes for a considerable distance. Transformation to pupæ takes place during the month of June. The moths appear in July. Both the male and the female insects have wings; but the female rarely flies. Pairing then takes place and egg deposition begins. The eggs then remain till the following spring, when they hatch and the same life cycle is repeated.

As in the case of the tussock moth, one of the most effective methods of keeping this pest under control is the careful collection and burning of the conspicuous egg masses. This can be done most effectively in the fall, during the winter and early spring. Creosote oil applied to the egg mass will soak in and kill the eggs. The following preparation was used in the work against the gipsy moth in Massachusetts: Creosote oil, 50 per cent., carbolic acid, 20 per cent., spirits of turpentine, 20 per cent., and coal-tar 10 per cent. The last was added to color the compound and thus show at a glance what clusters had been treated.

Advantage may be taken of the migrating habit of the caterpillar during the daytime by tying burlap bands around the tree-trunks and then turning down the upper portion of the burlap over the string. The bands can be lifted daily and the caterpillars beneath killed.

The larva is quite resistant to arsenical poison, and it requires a large dose to kill it. Arsenate of lead should be used as soon as the leaves are well grown, as the young caterpillars are most susceptible to the insecticide.

Brown Tail Moth (*Euproctis chrysorrhœa* Linn.).—The brown tail moth is the other species that has been introduced into Massachusetts within recent years and is scarcely second to the gipsy moth in destructiveness. About the middle of July the moths are on the wing, and each female lays from two hundred to three hundred eggs in an oblong cluster on the under side of the leaf, near the end of a branch, covering them with a dense mass of brown hair. The eggs hatch early in August. While still young the caterpillars make a nest in which they hibernate during the winter. This is constructed at the ends of the twigs and made by drawing together a few leaves, lining them with silk and surrounding them with a mass of silken threads. The tents are so firmly secured to the twigs that they can be removed only with considerable force.

The young caterpillars cease feeding and retire into these tents late in September, and there they remain during the winter in a sort of half-dormant condition. They become active again about the middle of April, or with the opening out of new foliage, and feed upon the buds and the unfolding leaves. They feed until June, when they spin an open cocoon of coarse silk among the leaves, and transform to pupæ. A month later the moths emerge to begin the life cycle again.

The brown tail moth attacks a great variety of both wild and cultivated plants, especially the oaks, maples, and elms. One of the ways of combating this species is by removing and burning the hibernating nests which are very conspicuous during the winter and in the spring. Spraying with arsenate of lead, both when the foliage develops and when the young caterpillars hatch, is also very effective.

Fall Webworm (*Hyphantria cunea* Dru.).—The presence of this insect can be readily discovered by the large tents formed by the caterpillars. The first brood is rarely abundant enough to attract attention, and the nests seem to be smaller than those found later in the season. Early in July the caterpillars are full grown, leave the nests and make cocoons in any convenient shelter near by, in crevices of the bark or on the surface of the ground. Moths issue in a few days and shortly afterward are ready to lay eggs in turn.

When the second brood appears in July, or early in August, the tents are so much more numerous that they attract more attention, and the insects grow so fast that unless measures are taken at once, the infested trees may suffer defoliation. Late in August and during the first half of September, the larvæ of the second brood leave the nests and wander to some shelter where they change to the pupal state and remain in that condition all winter.

The caterpillar of the fall webworm is a general feeder

PLATE 36.—FALL WEBWORM AND BAG WORM.

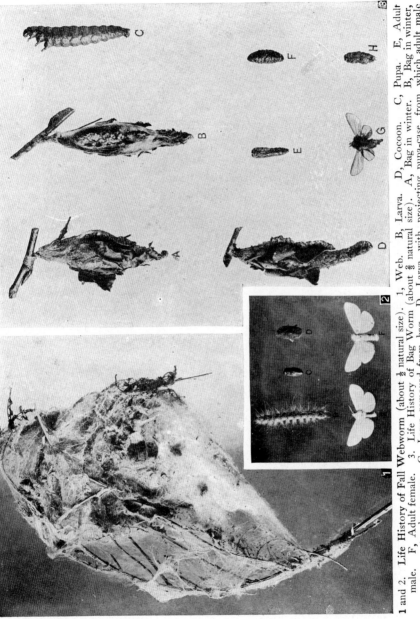

1 and 2. Life History of Fall Webworm (about ½ natural size). 1, Web. B, Larva. D, Cocoon. C, Pupa. E, Adult male. F, Adult female. 3. Life History of Bag Worm (about ⅔ natural size). A, Bag in winter. B, Bag in winter, cut open to show eggs. C, Larva removed from bag. D, Larva, with projecting pupa-case, from which adult male emerges. E, Maple pupa. F, Female pupa. G, Adult male. H, Adult female.

on many plants comprising fruit, shade, and ornamental trees. The easiest way to control the insect is to cut out the twigs having the nests of caterpillars and burn them. On large trees where the nests cannot be easily reached, the foliage at the points where the nests are observed should be sprayed with arsenate of lead. There is no necessity for spraying the entire tree, because the insects feed only in the immediate vicinity of the nest as long as there is any-thing to eat at that point. The earlier the spraying is done the more easily will the insects be destroyed.

Bag Worm (*Thyridopteryx ephemeræformis* Steph.).—This insect derives its name from the fact that the larva is pro-tected by a bag or case which it carries about as a shelter and in which it undergoes its transformations. In winter these bags are prominent objects on the leafless trees.

In May, the caterpillars develop, which after working out of the parent sack, at once begin to construct a bag of their own. At first the sack, which is just large enough to hold the insect, is carried upright; but as the larva increases in size and adds to the sack it becomes too heavy and is allowed to hang down, fastened to a twig or leaf by threads of silk when the insect is not actually moving.

The feeding on the foliage of the tree continues, and when full grown and ready to transform to the pupal stage, the larvæ become restless and wander to other trees. When a suitable place is found, the bags are attached to a twig or other support and the pupa is formed.

In about three weeks the male moth appears. The adult female is wingless and legless. She does not leave her case, but works out of it far enough to permit pairing, then returns into the pupal skin, fills it with eggs, and wriggles out of the bag and dies. The mouth of the bag closes after her and the eggs are thus securely protected until they are ready to hatch the ensuing spring.

The best way to control the pest is to pick off and burn the bags containing the egg masses during the winter. Spraying with arsenate of lead when the foliage develops is also effective.

Elm-Leaf Beetle (*Galerucella luteola* Müll.).—The winter of the elm-leaf beetle is passed in the adult condition, the beetles taking shelter in attics, sheds, out-houses, and other places. In the case of this insect, the adults also feed on the leaves. The beetles are about a quarter of an inch long and less than half that wide, dull yellow in color with a black stripe on each wing cover.

The adults emerge about the time the leaves begin to unfold and immediately begin to feed, eating irregular holes through the leaves. During the latter part of May and the beginning of June, eggs are deposited on the under side of the leaves. From these the larvæ hatch until the latter part of the month. The larvæ are about three-eighths or one-half inch long when full grown. They feed on the under-side of the leaves; but not through the tissue, and give the foliage a skeletonized appearance. Ordinarily their presence is not known until the larvæ are full grown, when the seriousness of the injury becomes apparent. The leaves turn brown, curl, and the entire tree looks as if a fire had swept through it.

Beginning during the last days of June and continuing until the middle of July, larvæ crawl down the trunks and change to yellow pupæ in the ground near the base of the tree. Adults develop about a week after the formation of the pupæ and in the latter part of July the summer brood of beetles is abundant.

PLATE 37.—LIFE HISTORY OF ELM-LEAF BEETLE.

1. Adult beetles eating holes through leaves after emerging from their hibernating quarters in the spring. 2. Egg mass on under side of leaf. 3. Larvæ feeding on under side of leaves, giving them a skeletonized appearance (1, 2, and 3 about ¾ natural size). 4. The curling of the foliage of the elm as a result of the feeding of the larvæ. 5. The contrast between sprayed and unsprayed elms attacked by the elm-leaf beetle. The tree on the left was sprayed with arsenate of lead May 20, 1909. The tree to the right, about 25 feet away, was not sprayed. View taken August 10, 1909.

Ordinarily there are two broods of this insect during a year. The beetles take to the leaves, feed on them and deposit their eggs. The larvæ of the second brood go through the same cycle of feeding on the under side of the leaves, changing to pupæ and transforming to adult beetles. In the latter part of August, the development of the second brood of beetles is complete. They hibernate during the winter in the adult form and begin to feed on the developing elm-leaves the following spring.

This insect is confined in its attacks to the elms, and prefers the European to the American variety. It has been a most serious pest in many States. The defoliation of a tree in midsummer is a serious injury, and if this occurs for successive years, the early death of the elm may be expected. Such has been the record of the elm-leaf beetle in a great many cities.

The only way to control the elm-leaf beetle is by spraying the foliage with arsenate of lead. The time to spray is just when the leaves develop and the adults begin to feed. A thorough spray at this time is very important, because if the beetles can be killed before they lay eggs, there will be no larvæ to deal with later.

If early spraying is neglected or has not been effective, an application of arsenate of lead is necessary when the larvæ begin to feed. It is important in this case to reach the under side of the leaves. The beetles eat the entire leaf tissue and it makes no difference whether the poison is on the under or upper surface. The larvæ eat only the lower layer of cells, and even if the upper surface be fully covered with arsenical poison they may not get even a particle.

When the full grown larvæ crawl down the trunks to

pupate, great numbers of them collect at the bases of the elm-trees. At that time they can be swept up and killed by pouring hot water on them. This, of course, is not a very effective measure; but still, it is helpful, and in order to secure the best results the grubs and the pupæ should be destroyed every few days so long as they are seen in numbers.

The elm-leaf beetle is now a serious pest in many Eastern States. The writer will therefore quote from his records of observations of the work against this pest in East Orange during 1909, as these will show approximately up to what time spraying can be effective. Corrections, of course, have to be made for variations in climate.

"The spraying began on May 18. On June 2, it was noticed that the depositing of eggs on the under side of the leaves had begun. The spraying, however, was continued during the period of incubation with good results. On June 10, it was noticed that the hatching of caterpillars had begun. On June 25, made an inspection of all the elms in the city. The early spraying was extremely effective. Some of the leaves were eaten by the adult beetles, but there were few egg masses. Spraying done after June 14 was also effective. Although the leaves showed many empty eggs, there were practically no larvæ, as these were poisoned as soon as they began to feed after hatching.

"On July 2, all spraying was stopped, as it was too late for spraying to be effective. On July 7, the caterpillars of the elm-leaf beetle were observed descending the trunks of the elm-trees to pupate. The devastating effect of the pest was then at its height. Not a single unsprayed tree within the city limits was free from the attack. Only a partial second brood of beetles was observed."

SUCKING INSECTS

Sucking insects eat no part of the plant itself, and it is absolutely impossible for that reason to kill them with any of the stomach poisons. They can be reached only by contact poisons which act on the breathing pores of the insects. Soaps and oils are the materials used, and these act by clogging up the spiracles of the insects and choking them.

Cottony Maple Scale (*Pulvinaria innumerabilis* Rathvon). —The cottony maple scale attacks all the maples to a certain extent, but is most injurious to the white maple. During the winter the hibernating females are found along the underside of the twigs and branches. They are oval, brown in color, and about one-sixteenth of an inch long. When the sap starts to flow in the spring the insects begin to feed and grow until they are about one-quarter inch long. In early June they excrete a mass of white, waxy, or cottony material in which the eggs are deposited. There are from one thousand to two thousand eggs in each mass. The larvæ hatch, crawl up on the leaves and settle along the veins on the under side. As many as a thousand settle on a single leaf and suck the sap as it comes up through the veins. In the meantime the waxy masses having served their purpose as a protection for the eggs, disintegrate, and the bits of white material are carried away by the winds. The pumping of the sap by the growing larvæ continues, the leaves become devitalized and about the latter part of July the foliage begins to fall as in late autumn.

The insects go through two or three molts and then change to pupæ. The mature male insects are winged, the female has no wings. In early September pairing takes place, the males die, the impregnated females remain on the

PLATE 38.—SCALE INSECTS.

1. The Woolly Maple Scale in cocoon condition, collected in masses in crevices of bark of Sugar Maple (about natural size). 2. Adult females of woolly maple scale surrounded by cottony tufts containing eggs. The larvæ are seen along the veins (about ½ natural size). 3. The Cottony Maple Scale, adult females on twig of white maple. The cottony masses excreted by them contain the eggs. 4. Twig infested by San José scale. 5. Twig infested by male scales of Scurfy Scale. 6. Twig infested by Oyster Shell Scale (3, 4, 5, and 6, about natural size).

leaves feeding until after the middle of September, when they migrate to the twigs and settle down to pass the winter.

It is very difficult to combat this pest. It has, however, a number of natural enemies which sometimes exterminate it before it does serious damage. The only time for carrying on spraying operations against the insect is during the fall and the winter, while the trees are in a dormant state. At that time any of the soluble oil preparations will be effective when used at winter strength.

There are many mechanical methods that can be used successfully in controlling this insect. Brushing with a stiff broom just where the white masses appear will destroy the eggs and prevent hatching. Small trees especially can be treated with very good results.

In 1904 and 1905, the Shade-Tree Commission of East Orange succeeded in controlling this pest by mechanical means. The trees were sprayed with water only, by directing a small solid jet from the power sprayer at the developing egg masses. A nozzle having a bore of about one-sixteenth of an inch was used and the water was discharged with sufficient pressure, so that when the stream was just drawn along the under side of the twigs it cleared it of egg clusters. The insects were dislodged and the egg masses broken up, so that the larvæ did not hatch.

Wherever city water pressure is available the insect may be combated by using a garden hose with a solid jet of water, and as the infestation is usually on the lower branches and on the under side, the method works in most cases.

Woolly Maple Scale (*Pseudococcus aceris* Sign.).—This insect, which attacks the sugar maple, passes the winter in the larval form. The larvæ are microscopic in size, collect in the crevices of the bark, and remain in a naked state all winter. In the latter part of May, when they change into the cocoon state, the presence of the pest is easily detected. The cocoons are about one-sixteenth of an inch long and perfectly white. On badly infested trees they are piled one on top of the other in such large numbers that the trunks look as if they had been whitewashed.

In early June the insects emerge from their cocoons. The females go up to the leaf and settle on the under side along the veins. They grow in size and surround themselves with a fluffy white mass and lay their eggs from which the young larvæ hatch. These scatter along the veins and suck the sap from the leaves. They begin to migrate during the latter part of July. They go along the petioles of the leaves, the main limbs, and gather on the trunks where they form their cocoons. During the latter part of July and early August the cocoons of the newly hatched larvæ begin to appear on the trees. Toward the end of August they leave the cocoons, pair, and then the females of the second brood again lodge themselves on the under side of the leaves to lay the eggs for the winter generation of larvæ. It is at this time that the infested sugar maples begin to lose their leaves.

Unlike other insects the several stages of metamorphosis of this one are not completed within the same time. While some of the insects are in cocoons others are already hatched and still others are laying eggs on the under side of the leaves. The additional fact that there are two broods a year during the summer, produces conditions making it possible to find the insect in all stages of development at any time in midsummer. These peculiarities make the treatment of the trees rather difficult, for the process that will destroy the larvæ or the adults will not hurt the eggs or the insects in cocoons.

The best way to control the pest is to wash the trunks of infested sugar maples with a solution of whale-oil soap at the rate of one pound to four gallons of water, or oil emulsion at weekly intervals from the middle of July until the leaves fall in late autumn. In early November, after the foliage is all gone, the trunks should be given a final treatment with the whale-oil soap or oil emulsion to kill the tiny larvæ that remain all winter. In that way the brood can be killed.

San José Scale (*Aspidiotus perniciosus* Comst.).—Although this species has been most destructive of fruit-trees, it attacks a large number of shade and ornamental trees as well. The twigs of badly infested trees, instead of being smooth and shiny, are covered with dark gray, scurfy patches that have a peculiar granular look which any one familiar with the bark of a rapidly growing tree will immediately recognize as not a normal condition.

The winter of the insect is passed in the half grown condition, covered by a round black scale about the size of a pin's head. During that season the insects do not feed and there is no drain upon the vitality of the tree. In May they resume growth. About the middle of June the young larvæ are born and begin to crawl from beneath the female insects. These young are minute, active, yellow atoms that crawl outwardly to the leaves and the young shoots. They insert their slender mouth-filaments into the plant tissue and begin to suck the sap. They change in form, become more circular, and very soon waxy filaments begin to ooze out all over the body, which form the scale. In about five or six weeks the species is mature, reproducing in turn, and by the end of the season the broods are no longer distinct, all stages occurring on infested trees at the same time.   A single pair, starting under favorable conditions in June, may have descendants to exceed one thousand million before snow is on the ground.

Experience has shown that the most effective way to control the San José Scale is to spray with oil or soap emulsions as soon after the middle of October as possible.   At that time, the functions of the leaves have been accomplished and any scorching of the foliage by the spray will not affect the tree itself.   It is best to choose a sunshiny day for the work, to use a nozzle that will give a fine spray and to apply the mixture until the twigs begin to drip.

Scurfy Scale (*Chionaspis furfurus* Fitch).—This scale usually infests the poplars and the maples among the shade-trees.   It is a very pale gray, almost as broad as long, with a yellowish point or head.   Beneath this scale the eggs are found during the winter, and in June they hatch into purplish-colored larvæ, which suck the plant juices.   There is only a single brood which matures in September, and is rarely abundant enough to do very much injury.

This scale is thinner than most others of the armored forms, and may be reached by caustic sprays in the winter. If no winter application is made it is necessary to wait until the eggs hatch in June, and then apply whale-oil soap or kerosene emulsion.

Oyster-Shell Scale (*Mytilaspis pomorum* Bouché).—Like the San José scale this insect attacks orchard-trees mostly, but is also present on shade-trees.   It derives its name from the resemblance to one of the very elongate types of oysters. It winters in the egg state under the scale, and in May or June the eggs hatch into minute yellow atoms that set and begin to form small scales.   These suck the juices of the twigs and increase in size until midsummer, or a little later. Then the males mature, and the females, after impregnation, lay their eggs, which fill the space beneath the scale. Sometimes there are two broods during the season.

There is only one period during which this insect can be satisfactorily reached; that is, when the eggs have hatched and while the larvæ are moving about or have just set. This is during late May or early June. As soon as the larvæ are observed, spray with whale-oil soap at the rate of one pound to five gallons of water, or kerosene emulsion. Repeat, if possible, a week later to reach delayed larvæ.

Plant Lice.—Most shade-trees suffer from plant lice to a greater or less extent; but none more than the Norway maple. These insects multiply very rapidly, suck the juices of the leaves and shoots, and so exhaust their vitality. When the insects become abundant the honey dew excreted by them sometimes covers the leaves with a sticky secretion that may be abundant enough to drop to the street below. This secretion tends to clog the foliage so that it may drop while yet perfectly green, and a black soot fungus is also likely to develop.

Plant lice are most abundant during a cold, wet spring, and the attack usually does not continue after the first spell of hot dry weather; so that treatment is generally not found necessary.

Should spraying be desirable nothing is better against plant lice than whale-oil soap at the rate of one pound to five gallons of water.

BORERS

Besides the leaf-eating and the sucking insects that injure trees through defoliation, shade-trees are also subject to the attacks of borers that feed on their wood tissue. As soon as the larvæ of these insects hatch they bore their way through the bark into the wood and make a series of galleries either immediately beneath the bark or deeper in the tree.   In these they develop and emerge as winged insects.

Leopard Moth (*Zeuzera pyrina* Fabr.).—The most destructive species on city trees is the leopard moth.   Practically all kinds of shade-trees are attacked by the larva. During the latter days of June and in early July the adult insects are most abundant.   The eggs are deposited by the females either singly or in masses, a single adult depositing between five hundred and one thousand eggs.   They are usually placed in a bark crevice or other sheltered situation on one of the small twigs or branches.   On hatching, the young caterpillar makes its way to the crotch of a small branch or bud and at once bores into the wood tissue.

It works downward toward the base, and grows very rapidly.   Presently it leaves its burrow and wanders to a large branch and again begins feeding.   The caterpillars bore a straight channel through the centre of the branch or eat out a large cavity on one side of it.   Many of the caterpillars gnaw an irregular chamber of the size of a man's hand right under the bark.

Two years are required to complete the life cycle.   By the end of the first season the larva is half-grown and has usually made its way to one of the large branches.

The caterpillars remain in the dormant state during the winter and resume feeding the next spring.   During the second summer, growth is rapid, and at the end of the season the larvæ reach their full size of two inches or more.   In that state they pass the second winter, and early in the spring following work close to the surface and form pupæ from which the adult moths emerge.

PLATE 39.—BORERS.

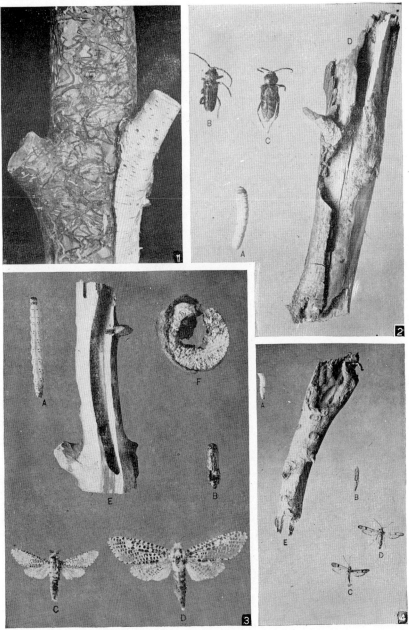

1. Bronze Birch Borer, Galleries in inner bark of White Birch made by larvæ (about ⅛ natural size).
2. Life History of Sugar Maple Borer (about ½ natural size). A, Larva. B, Adult male. C, Adult female. D, Galleries made by larvæ. 3. Life History of Leopard Moth (about ⅔ natural size). A, Larva. B, Pupa. C, Adult male. D, Adult female. E and F, Galleries made by larvæ. 4. Life History of Maple Tree Sesiid (about ½ natural size). A, Larva. B, Pupa. C, Adult male. D, Adult female. E, Galleries made by larvæ.

The injuries to trees by borers are very severe. When they girdle a limb the effect is immediate. The circulation of the sap is cut off from the end of the branch and it soon dies. When a large wound is made on the side of a branch, the bark covering it breaks away, the wood is exposed, it dries and checks, the successive annual layers do not cover up the scar, so that in time the circulation of the sap is retarded and the end of the limb dies. The injury to the trees in that case is not immediately apparent, but is none the less fatal.

The leopard moth is hard to combat. The moths do not feed and the caterpillars feed on the surface only for a short time, when they change their quarters and start in a new place. At the end of July and during August the larvæ force great strings of partly digested wood or "sawdust" through the openings by which they entered. At that time they can be readily killed by injecting through the openings of the burrows a few drops of bisulfid of carbon and closing them with putty.

When the trees of a city are attacked by borers it would seem that the task of combating them is almost hopeless. Persistence will yield results, however. On August 20, 1909, for example, the Shade-Tree Commission of East Orange began work against the leopard moth. By September 22, about eight thousand trees were treated by a gang of six men. Two methods were used to kill the borers; by injecting carbon bisulfid into the burrow and plugging the opening with putty, and also by using a wire. The latter method was found to be more rapid. Badly infested small branches were entirely removed.

In this work it was possible to cover only the trunks and the main limbs of the trees. The men could not reach the ends of the branches and small twigs where the newly hatched larvæ are found. The work done, however, was effective, as the caterpillars that would have matured by the following spring were killed and thus the deposition of eggs for another brood was almost entirely prevented. In the summer of 1910, when the overwintering larvæ began their borings farther down the trees, the work of killing these was carried on in the same way as during the summer of 1909. In that way the entire brood of borers was exterminated as thoroughly as it was possible.

Sugar Maple Borer (*Plagionotus speciosus* Say).—Sugar maples on streets and roadsides have no more serious enemy than the sugar maple borer, which, unlike other borers, attacks trees in full vigor. Like the leopard moth this insect takes two years to complete its growth. At the end of the first season the larva is partly grown. It passes the winter in that condition, resumes feeding and growth the following summer, hibernates as a full grown larva the second winter, and in the spring after that changes into a pupa and then emerges as a beetle.

Constant watchfulness is needed to detect the presence of this borer. Each fall and spring sugar maples should be examined for characteristic signs of borings. The pest can be exterminated in the same way as the leopard moth.

Maple Tree Sesiid (*Sesia acerni* Clem.).—This is another caterpillar borer found in soft and hard maples. It has a special fondness for tissues growing over wounds in which it makes round holes not over one-eighth of an inch in diameter. Trees wounded from any causes find difficulty in covering the exposed wood with bark after being attacked by this insect.

The injuries caused by this borer are not so serious as

those of the former.   The caterpillars bore near the surface and are easily dug out and destroyed.   Where the insects are observed in great numbers it will pay to whitewash the trunks several times during the season.   This will repel the moths that would otherwise deposit on the trunks, and it would cover over or partly fill the small holes that have been made by the insects.

Bark Borers.—Some borers which attack trees work in the cambium layer just under the bark, making a series of galleries which interlace each other and extend all the way around the branches of infected trees.

The effect of these borings is slow girdling.   The circulation of sap is cut off and the upper part of the branches die.

Some of the more common bark borers attacking shade and ornamental trees are the bronze birch borer (*Agrilus anxius* Gory.), which attacks the various species of birch, the two-lined chestnut borer (*Agrilus bilineatus* Weber), which infests the chestnut and the oak, and the hickory-bark borer (*Scolytus quadrispinosus* Say), which is most injurious to the hickory.

The cutting out of infested branches sometimes checks the disease if it has not spread far down to the trunk.   In the majority of cases, however, there is no remedy for trees once attacked by these borers.

FUNGOUS DISEASES

Many diseases of trees are caused by low forms of vegetable life, known as fungi, which live upon and within the tissues of the higher plants.   They possess none of the green coloring matter of ordinary vegetation and are made dependent upon the organic matter prepared by green plants.   They are thus parasites which obtain their nourishment by the breaking down of the cells of the plants on which they exist.

As affecting shade-trees the fungous diseases are not so serious as the injuries by insects.   Very few wood-rotting fungi are capable of entering an injured tree and beginning growth.   Nearly all gain lodgment in wounds, grow in these and rot the wood.   Fungous diseases, therefore, are usually the result of some form of neglect, and it is the preventive measures rather than the cures that count for most in maintaining the health of trees.   The various types of fungi will therefore be mentioned only briefly.

WOOD-DESTROYING FUNGI

The most familiar fungi are the shelving or bracket forms seen on dead or decaying trees.   These shelves or brackets are the fruit bodies, which on maturity liberate millions of spores for the reproduction of other plants.   The spores, which are unicellular, microscopic bodies corresponding to the seeds of higher plants, are scattered by the wind and find lodgment in wounds of trees, where they begin to sprout.   They grow unseen for a long time by threadlike roots called hyphæ which bore through and between the cell-walls forming a mass of white meshes called the mycelium. This spreads through the heart of the tree, rapidly disintegrates the wood and causes it to rot.

When the mycelium has spread over a large feeding area and has stored reserve food it can then grow out through a wound or old knot-hole and form the bracket fruit body.

False-Tinder Fungus (*Pyropolyporus igniarius* (Linn.) Murrill) (*Fomes igniarius* (Linn.) Gillet).––The fungi which are responsible for the decay and destruction of the heart-wood of various broad-leaf trees are quite numerous.   They

PLATE 40.—FUNGOUS DISEASES.

1. Living Apple with fruiting body of False-Tinder Fungus (*Pyropolyporus igniarius*). 2. Cross-section of living Beech diseased by *Pyropolyporus igniarius*. Fruiting body is seen on the outside. 3. Living Sugar Maple with fruiting bodies of *Hydnum septentrionale* causing Heart-Rot of Sugar Maple. 4. Cross-section of same Sugar Maple as 3, two feet above fruiting bodies, showing centre rotted by mycelium of *Hydnum septentrionale*. 5. White Oak, with fruiting body of *Dædalea quercina* growing out of a knot-hole. 6. A longitudinal and transverse section of the white oak in 5, two feet below fruiting body, showing the disintegration of the wood by the mycelium of *Dædalea quercina*.

are more or less alike, however, in their manner of entrance into the trees, their subsequent development, the production of their fruiting bodies, and general remedies. The false-tinder fungus may be taken as a type of this class of fungi. Among the trees it is known to attack are the following species: the beech, the aspen, the willows, the sugar, the red, the silver and the striped maples, the oaks, the apple, and the hickory.

The disease caused by this fungus is commonly known as "white heart-rot." It is usually confined to the heart-wood of the tree. This is changed by the growth and development of the mycelium, into a whitish, soft substance, which is bounded from the healthy wood by very thin black layers. These show as black lines when the trunk of the tree is sawn across. The fungus gains entrance into the trunk of the tree through some wound. In a majority of cases infection takes place through old branch stubs. The spores germinate on a stub, and the hyphæ grow down through the wood of a stub until they reach the heart-wood of the main trunk. The destruction of the wood follows very shortly after the entrance of the mycelium into the trunk, progressing outward and up and down as long as the tree lives.

The formation of the fruiting bodies takes place usually at the point where infection originally occurred. A tree attacked by the fungus shows no particular change in its general external appearance during the early stages of the disease; in fact, it is practically impossible to recognize a diseased tree until the fruiting bodies of the fungus form on the outside of the trunk. When the fruiting bodies appear it may be taken for granted that the disease has progressed within the trunk in both directions for two or three feet from the point of infection. As the disease progresses new fruiting bodies appear and the older ones grow in size.   The rotting of the heart-wood continues until the tree, checked in growth and become a mere shell of weak sapwood, is broken off by a windstorm and its existence terminated.

There is no cure for diseases caused by wound parasites after the fungi enter into the interior of the tree.   For a few years there may be no apparent injury, but with the lapse of time the tree becomes badly decayed if not destroyed. The only practical measures of controlling these fungi are of a preventive nature.   All broken and dead branches of trees should be removed as quickly as possible, and all wounds, either natural or as a result of pruning, should be covered with tar.   The destruction of the fruiting bodies as they appear helps to check the spread of the diseases.

Sulfur Polyporus (*Lætiporus speciosus* (Batt.) Murrill) (*Polyporus sulphureus* (Bul.) Fr.).—The sulfur polyporus has a very wide distribution, and is important because it is found chiefly on the oaks.   It also occurs on the apple, ash, birch, butternut, hemlock, locust, and pine.   It is a wound parasite like the false-tinder fungus, and grows on living trees.   The mycelium rots the heart of the tree and the fruit bodies grow from knot-holes, and also arise from portions of the trunk killed by the fungus.

The sulfur polyporus is easy to recognize because of the yellowish color of the soft, spore-bearing bodies.   They form a series of shelves overlapping one another.   Sometimes they form very close together, so as to produce a large, round mass about the size of a person's head.   The fruiting bodies of this fungus rarely remain on the tree for any length of time, because they are attacked by insects which destroy them.   The fungus is also eagerly sought by mushroom hunters on account of its excellent edible qualities.

The effect of the destruction of the heart-wood of trees brought about by this fungus is of a nature resembling the decay caused by the false-tinder fungus; and what has been said regarding methods of control of the latter applies to this species as well.

Heart-Rot of Sugar Maple (*Hydnum septentrionale* Fr.). —This fungus is found principally on the sugar maple; but also on other species of deciduous trees. The effects of this fungus upon the wood of diseased trees produces a heart decay similar to that of the false-tinder fungus.

The color of the sporophores is creamy white, and they appear in bracketlike clusters that have a striking appearance.

SAP-ROTS OF TREES

In the economy of nature many fungi serve a useful purpose in breaking down dead wood and clearing the forest of débris. Fungi which grow only on dead wood are saprophytic, while those which feed on living tissue are parasitic. Frequently no sharp line can be drawn between those fungi which are capable of growing on dead wood that has died after being cut from a living tree and the fungi which grow on dead wood of the still living tree. Some of these fungi are mentioned in this connection because they are frequently taken to be the cause of disease.

The Common Bracket Fungus (*Elfvingia megaloma* (Lév.) Murrill) (*Fomes applanatus* (Pers.) Wallr.) may be taken as a type of this class of fungi. It is frequently found on living trees, but a careful examination always shows it to be growing on wood which is actually dead. Generally this is the outer sapwood. The sporophores or fruiting bodies of this fungus constitute brackets. The upper surface is more or less marked by concentric zones which divide off

PLATE 41.—FUNGOUS AND OTHER DISEASES.

1. Partly dead Sugar Maple with fruiting bodies of sap-rot fungus, *Elfvingia megaloma*.
2. "Stag-head" White Maple.   3. Ulcers on Red Maple, suffering from gas-poisoning.
4. Fruiting bodies of Sulfur Polyporus (after illustration, Bulletin 149, Bureau of Plant Industry, U. S. Department of Agriculture).   5. Leaf scorch of Sugar Maple.   6. Leaf of European Linden, spotted by the Linden Rust, caused by *Cercospora microsora*.   7. Leaf of Horse-chestnut curled as a result of Leaf Spot, caused by *Phyllosticta paviæ*.   8. Partly dead Red Maple with fruiting bodies of the sap-rot fungus *Hopalopili gilvus*.

the growth of the different years. The fruiting surface is white, and when bruised turns brown, and hence the brackets of this species are used for sketching.

A sap-rot fungus frequently found on city trees is *Hopalopilus gilvus* (Schw.) Murrill (*Polyporus gilvus* Schw.). It has no common name and is classed with the ordinary polypores that live on decayed wood.

One of the most important enemies of structural oaks and chestnuts is *Dædalea quercina* (Linn.) Pers. It is generally found on oak and chestnut logs, ties, telegraph-poles, fences, etc., all of which it destroys with rapidity. This fungus also occurs on dead portions of living trees, and the sporophores may be found growing out from large wounds.

ROOT-ROTS

The roots of trees are also subject to diseases of which the rotting caused by the honey agaric (*Armillaria mellea* Vahl.) is an example. The fungus usually gains entrance through some wound in the root system. The young mycelium grows into the cambium layer, attacks the living cells, and finally completely encircles the base of the trunk of an affected tree. The most characteristic parts of the honey agaric are the hard black strands popularly known as "shoe strings," which extend in all directions through the ground and along the roots of affected trees.

The danger of any root-rotting disease lies in the fact that trees so affected are liable to be blown down without warning. Such rots as gain entrance through wounds at the base of the trunk can be prevented by properly treating all abrasions of the bark; but other forms of the disease, including the case of the honey agaric, spread through the ground and are difficult to prevent. Careful inspection of such trees, however, will reveal the disease, and they can be cut down before they become dangerous. If the trees are not blown down they usually die suddenly in early summer, the foliage wilting completely.

CANKER

Diseases of the bark of trees manifest themselves by the appearance of small protuberances and other malformations commonly known as canker. The disease is due to fungi, one of the most destructive of which is *Nectria cinnabarina* (Tode) Fr. Its spores obtain entrance into wounds caused by hailstones, insects, or breakages, and the mycelium grows through the partially weakened wood, and ultimately produces small red clusters of fruiting bodies. A small area of the bark is killed and a healing callus begins to form at the edge of the wound. The callus of the first year is then invaded by the fungus and killed, and a second layer of callus starts to develop. The continuation of this process extends the growth of the canker over a large area.

Canker can be treated by cutting away all diseased portions of wood and bark, washing the exposed surface with a solution of copper sulfate, one pound to five gallons of water, and then painting the same with coal-tar.

The chestnut bark disease or canker (*Diaporthe parasitica* Murrill) is now the most serious of all the fungous diseases of trees. The spores enter the bark through an abrasion or some other wound. From the point of infection the fungus grows, kills a small patch of bark, and then spreads all around the limb or trunk and girdles it. The disease then becomes conspicuous by the brown color of the dying foliage. The branches are usually attacked first, and from these the canker spreads through the entire tree and kills it.

Up to the present time no means has been discovered of successfully combating this pest.

LEAF DISEASES

Shade-trees sometimes suffer from diseases which affect the foliage. The assimulating area of the leaves is thus reduced, and the growth of the tree is diminished in proportion to the leaf area destroyed. While ordinarily they check the growth of the trees for one season only, if the disease appears several years in succession it may seriously weaken and even kill the tree.

Diseases of the foliage can be controlled by timely spraying. The germination of fungi may be prevented by the use of mineral salts. Those of copper are more commonly used, especially the sulfate, usually in the form of Bordeaux mixture (see page 207). Just as long as leaves or other tissues of plants are covered with a thin coating of Bordeaux mixture, no fungi can develop upon them. Thus a fungicide is a preventive, and its application should begin long before the disease has advanced far enough to manifest itself to any extent.

Rusts.—This term has been applied in more or less of an arbitrary manner to a large group of fungi that produce masses of spores on the surface of the leaves, generally yellowish or brownish in color. The linden rust (*Cercospora microsora* Sacc.) may be taken as an example. Leaves attacked by this fungus become badly spotted, and the margins decayed and tattered.

Spraying the branches thoroughly with copper sulfate, one pound to twenty-five gallons, or strong Bordeaux mixture, before the leaves unfold, will destroy all of the earlier spores upon them. Then if the trees are where the Bordeaux mixture will not be too conspicuous, it may be applied at intervals of from two to four weeks during July and August. If the trees are in a very conspicuous place, the dilute copper sulfate, one pound to two hundred and fifty or three hundred gallons, may be used, as often as every two weeks and after heavy rains. The great advantage of Bordeaux mixture is that it holds the copper firmly to the leaves and with every rain or heavy dew, minute quantities are dissolved and the spores are prevented from germinating.

Mildews.—These are parasites which produce white spores and more or less white patches on the leaf or other parts. The powdery mildew of the willow (*Uncinula salicis* (DeC.) Wint.) and the mildew occurring on some species of maple (*Uncinula aceris* (DeC.) Wint.) may be taken as examples. Coming on later in the season than the brown rusts, two or three applications of either the Bordeaux mixture or dilute copper sulfate will be effectual, but no application need be made generally until the middle or last of July.

Blights.—The leaf blights are unlike the rusts in that they attack and destroy small portions of the leaves, and when these spots or places become numerous the whole leaf is destroyed and it soon falls off.

The leaf spot of the horse-chestnut and the sycamore leaf blight are two of the most destructive leaf diseases of this class.

The destructive work of the leaf spot of the horse-chestnut (*Phyllosticta paviæ* Desm.) becomes conspicuous early in the season by the appearance of small brown spots on the leaflets; these spread to a large size and produce dead areas of curled and broken tissue until the foliage becomes ragged. This is followed by early defoliation of the trees.

The leaf spot can be controlled by spraying in winter with copper sulfate solution to destroy the spores lodged in the bark. This should be followed by applications of Bordeaux mixture once before the flowers appear and two or three times thereafter at intervals of about two weeks.

The sycamore leaf blight (*Glœosporeum nervisequum* Sacc.) needs particular mention. It attacks both the European and the American species, but the native variety, *Platanus occidentalis*, seems to be more susceptible. It develops with great rapidity at the time of the development of the foliage in the spring, and causes the leaves to hang lifeless upon the stems. In severe cases the leaves are dropped prematurely, and if the attacks are continued for several years the trees become seriously weakened.

This trouble can be controlled by raking up and burning loose bark, dead branches and leaves, and spraying with Bordeaux mixture. The spraying should be done during the resting period of the trees, as the leaves begin to develop, ten days later and within three weeks of the time of the unfolding of the buds.

DISEASES DUE TO CONDITIONS OF SOIL AND CLIMATE

Diseases due to insects and fungi are more easy of diagnosis than those due to unfavorable surroundings. Sometimes, however, no sharp line can be drawn between the two classes of diseases. As long as the conditions for obtaining food and water from the soil and for conducting these to every part of the tree are favorable and the effects of climate are not detrimental to growth, the tree will continue to be in full vigor. If, on the contrary, there be a continual drain on the supply of soil-foods with no addition, and there be long periods of drought, severe cold or other unfavorable climatic conditions, the tree will become so weakened that it will succumb to the attacks of parasites.

By examining a tree carefully and noting its condition as compared with other trees of the same species known to be in a state of full vigor, one may determine whether the specimen is in a good state of health or not. The points to consider are generally the following: the growth in height as shown by the vigor and length of the shoots; the growth of the trunk in diameter; the color and mass of the foliage; the time of the unfolding and shedding of the leaves; the development of the crown, whether regular in all its parts; and the mode of shedding of the foliage, whether simultaneous in all parts of the tree.

Soil Conditions.—There is no doubt that in the case of city trees, causes of decay and death can in the majority of cases, be traced to poor conditions of the soil, such as lack of food and water and root suffocation.

A disease known as "stag-head" or "top dry" frequently results from lack of proper food in the soil, and manifests itself by the gradual death of the top of the tree. Where trees grow year after year and there is no addition to the available soil foods, and where the earth is dried out by the sun and grass, starvation necessarily follows. The tree, therefore, gradually stops growing, the branches slowly die, and other diseases set in, until finally the last branch is dead.

A constant supply of proper food is necessary to prevent this disease. The ground underneath the tree should not be sodded. It should be worked and top dressed at frequent intervals to keep up the food-supply.

Imperfect circulation of air in the soil has an important bearing on the health of trees. City trees are likely to suffer a lack of aeration of the soil, because of pavements and walks. The use of grills and the keeping of the soil loose will help the exchange of gases between the soil atmosphere and the air.

Root asphyxiation is especially liable to occur along streets where the ground water is only a few feet from the surface. During prolonged rainy weather the water rises, making the soil wet up close to the surface. The pavement adds here to the evil of poor under-drainage, preventing evaporation and aeration.

Young trees set too deep are often killed, and covering the earth about trees with soil a foot or more deep usually results in injury, if not death from asphyxiation.

Ulcers.—This general term will be made to include all internal injuries and diseases which manifest themselves externally by the flow of sap over the bark. A disease known as slime-flux is characterized by the appearance of various colored slimy masses with a decidedly acid odor which start at or near wounds. They make their appearance usually in the spring when the sap, containing more or less sugar, flows from the wounds. In the sap a number of forms of algæ, bacteria, and fungi begin to grow and form a slimy, dripping mass over the bark. The cambium beneath dies rapidly, and if the disease is not checked the destruction may extend completely around a tree, resulting in the death of branches and sometimes of the entire tree.

An exudation of sap sometimes occurs through splits in the bark, not near any wounds, and which from the outside appears to be perfectly normal and healthy. The liquid is usually mucilaginous and fermented, and as it flows over the bark it discolors it gray, brown, or reddish. The species on which such a condition is most frequently noticed are horse-chestnuts, elms, maples, poplars, and oaks.

The writer once had under observation a number of trees suffering from gas-poisoning.   There were elms, Norway maples, sugar maples, white maples, and red maples among them.   About the time when the red and the white maples began to show the usual symptoms of the poison, such as the etiolation and the partial loss of the foliage, the sap began to ooze out from a number of places on the trunk and main branches.   The sap did not come from openings made by borers or other causes, but through splits of bark looking normal on the outside.   On removing the bark there was seen a discoloration of the sap-wood, and the descending current of sap flowed freely near the point of this discoloration. If a part only of the bark covering this diseased spot was cut away, the sap was seen coming out from under the portion of the bark still covering the remainder of this blister-like formation.   The sap flowing from the splits in the bark was frothy white in appearance (Plate 41, Fig. 3), and had a fermented odor, as that of cider.

The exact cause and nature of the formation of ulcers in trees is not yet fully understood.   The condition is variously ascribed to an excess of humidity in the soil, to sudden changes of temperature during the growing season, to the non-utilization of all the sap for growth, to a decomposition of internal tissues, and to a modification of the chemical composition of the sap.   There is no doubt, however, that the disease is due to a general disturbance of the nutrition of the tree which is followed by local fermentation of bark areas.

The division of Forest Pathology of the Bureau of Plant Industry of the United States Department of Agriculture, expects to undertake within a few years systematic work on phenomena of the class to which ulcers and slime-flux belong.

Ulcers can be treated by making vertical incisions in the bark near the wound to allow the liquid to flow off as rapidly as possible and, when the current stops, cutting away the diseased bark and painting with coal-tar.

Drying Out and Leaf Scorch.—Young leaves and sometimes tender shoots which have pushed out during a spell of cold or cloudy weather frequently wither and die, when exposed to bright, hot sun. The trouble usually occurs when a rather moist spring, favorable to growth, is followed by dry and very hot weather.

Remedial measures are not always easy to carry out, but the harm may be lessened by any treatment that keeps the soil moist and aerated, so that the foliage may have an ample supply of water to draw upon.

Frequently there is much complaint of the leaves of many trees, especially sugar maples, being affected with an apparent disease that causes a loss of green in those parts most distant from the main veins. The trouble has been studied at several experiment stations, and the consensus of opinion is that it is of physiological origin. A lack of water-supply to the leaf tissue causes the death of the least resistant portions of the leaf during a hot and dry spell.

The writer has found that such a condition can generally be remedied by the mulching of trees in the fall, keeping the soil loose and watering freely.

Frost.—The injuries from freezing are of a nature similar to drying. Freezing of the plant tissues in fact is the drying out of the water which they contain. If the tissues are dried beyond the point where they are able to take up water again, they are killed. In general, trees native to a given section resist injuries of this sort. In the case of trees introduced from warmer regions care has to be exercised in their location and protection from frosts.

Smooth barked trees sometimes have their trunks and larger branches injured on the southwest side during the winter, the injuries being characterized by the death of patches of bark. During the latter part of winter and early spring, when there are periods of several days of warm weather, the cambium on the south side of the trunk and larger limbs is stimulated to premature activity. If the warm spell is followed by freezing weather these partially active areas are killed. After a time the bark separates from the wood and splits. The injury does not manifest itself until well into the summer. The dead tissue forms a favorable place for the growth of parasites that cause the rotting of the wood.

Trees can be protected from injuries caused by alternate freezing and thawing by wrapping with burlap or straw. When injuries have been produced the affected areas should be cut away and painted with tar.

CHAPTER IX

INSECTICIDES, FUNGICIDES, AND SPRAYING

INSECTICIDES

INSECTICIDES are of two general types, those that kill by being eaten, or stomach poisons; and those that kill by actually touching the insects, or contact poisons. The distinction is an important one. Insects that eat up the foliage can be killed by applying to the leaves some mixture containing arsenic. Insects that suck the juices of a plant are safe from all poisons because no poison can be got into their food. They make a minute puncture in the leaf-tissue and then pump the sap, and get none of the poison. Such insects must be killed by a contact poison which must cover them and corrode their tissues, or choke them by clogging their breathing pores.

Stomach Poisons.—Against those insects that feed upon plant tissue there is nothing better than arsenic in some form. Paris green, which contains about 50 per cent. of arsenic, has been frequently employed; but the safest arsenical poison for spraying trees is arsenate of lead. Its use has become quite common during the last few years. Paris green is an effective insecticide, but is liable to injure the foliage. Arsenate of lead is effective against insects and is harmless to foliage when used at any reasonable strength. It remains in suspension longer than Paris green, and adheres to the foliage a longer time than any other stomach poison.

When sprayed in midsummer, leaves retain some of the arsenate of lead when they fall in autumn.

Arsenate of lead may be prepared as follows:

Acetate of lead..........................12 oz.
Arsenate of soda........................ 4 oz.
Water......................15 to 20 gallons.

Pour the acetate of lead into two quarts of water and the arsenate of soda into another two quarts; then pour these two solutions into a tank containing fifteen or twenty gallons of water. This gives a white precipitate of arsenate of lead. Good chemicals should be used.

It very seldom pays in actual spraying operations to prepare the arsenate of lead. It is best to buy it in paste form ready made. The manufacture of insecticides has become more general during the last few years, and with the passage of the National Insecticide Law their adulteration will be prevented. This law is known as "The Insecticide Act of 1910," and came into effect January 1, 1911. It is "an act for preventing the manufacture, sale, or transportation of adulterated or misbranded Paris greens, lead arsenates, and other insecticides, and also fungicides, and for regulating traffic therein, and for other purposes." The standards of strength and purity of insecticides and fungicides are prescribed in section 7 of the act, which is as follows:

"SEC. 7. That for the purpose of this Act an article shall be deemed to be adulterated—

"In the case of Paris green: First, if it does not contain at least fifty per centum of arsenious oxid; second, if it contains arsenic in water-soluble forms equivalent to more than three and one-half per centum of arsenious oxid;

third, if any substance has been mixed and packed with it so as to reduce or lower or injuriously affect its quality or strength.

"In the case of lead arsenate: First, if it contains more than fifty per centum of water; second, if it contains total arsenic equivalent to less than twelve and one-half per centum of arsenic oxid (As_2O_5); third, if it contains arsenic in water-soluble forms equivalent to more than seventy-five one-hundredths per centum of arsenic oxid (As_2O_5); fourth, if any substances have been mixed and packed with it so to reduce, lower, or injuriously affect its quality or strength: *Provided, however,* That extra water may be added to lead arsenate (as described in this paragraph) if the resulting mixture is labeled lead arsenate and water, the percentage of extra water being plainly and correctly stated on the label.

"In the case of insecticides or fungicides other than Paris green and lead arsenate: First, if its strength or purity fall below the professed standard or quality under which it is sold; second, if any substance has been substituted wholly or in part for the article; third, if any valuable constituent of the article has been wholly or in part abstracted; fourth, if it is intended for use on vegetation and shall contain any substance or substances which, although preventing, destroying, repelling, or mitigating insects, shall be injurious to such vegetation when used."

Contact Poisons.—Whale-oil soap, which is a common name for all fish-oil soaps now on the market, is the simplest contact insecticide, especially if only a few trees are to be sprayed. Used at the rate of one pound in from four to six gallons of water in the summer-time it will kill plant lice and other sucking insects. At the rate of one pound in two gallons of water it can be used on dormant trees for winter washes to kill the cottony maple scale or the woolly maple scale.

Kerosene emulsion is one of the most common contact insecticides. A 10 per cent. solution of kerosene in water is the usual strength employed in spraying foliage with safety. Kerosene and water alone do not emulsify, and if an attempt is made to spray with only a mechanical mixture of the oil and water, the chances are that neither pure oil nor water is pumped at any one time. Soap is therefore added to the oil in order to make an emulsion.

The preparation is made as follows:

Kerosene............................2 gals.
Soap...............................$\frac{1}{2}$ lb.
Water...............................1 gal.

Dissolve the soap in hot water, add the kerosene and churn thoroughly, or pump into itself till a creamy emulsion is formed. This emulsion, diluted with from twelve to fifteen times its own bulk of water, is an excellent summer remedy for plant lice and other soft-bodied insects that can be reached with contact poisons.

There are now soft soaps on the market by means of which it is possible to emulsify kerosene with water without heating any of the ingredients. The soap is dissolved in the water and then the kerosene is added while the mixture is being pumped into itself until an emulsion is formed.

There are also many oil and petroleum preparations now manufactured that are soluble in cold water and are ready for use on mixing. A perfect emulsion is formed without pumping, and no stirring is necessary while the mixture is being applied. These miscible oils are rather expensive, but have the advantage of being always ready for use. To the owner of a few trees nothing better could be recommended. For extensive spraying the use of miscible oils will usually be found advisable also. The time and labor necessary to prepare the oil emulsions bring their cost up to an amount equal to or greater than that of the soluble oils.

Vapors.—The vapor of bisulfid of carbon is used in killing borers. The liquid is injected into the burrow with an oil-can or syringe, and the opening plugged with putty. The fumes given off by the carbon bisulfid are fatal to all insects that breathe it. Carbon bisulfid is very inflammable.

FUNGICIDES

Fungicides act as preventives of plant disease by obstructing the germination of the spores of the fungi causing such disease. If the leaves of trees, for example, are covered with a coating of copper sulfate or other chemical deleterious to the germination of the spores, the reproduction of the fungi is held in check and disease prevented.

Bordeaux Mixture.—This is the standard fungicide and consists of a combination of copper sulfate, fresh lime, and water. The formula in most general use is the following:

Copper sulfate......................... 4 lbs.
Fresh lime............................. 4 lbs.
Water to make ....50 gals.

By combining the copper and the lime it is found that the copper sulfate may be used more freely and with less injury than if used alone, and it will adhere a long time to the foliage. For preparing this fungicide on a small scale, the copper sulfate should be dissolved in twenty-five gallons of water, using a half barrel for the purpose. To dissolve the copper sulfate readily, it should be placed in a coarse cloth bag and suspended in the water so that the salt is just covered. The lime should be dissolved in another vessel, using only a small amount of water at first, adding more as the process of slacking progresses, and then diluting to twenty-five gallons. The copper sulfate solution and the milk of lime should then be poured into a third vessel. It is best to strain the materials when pouring them together. It is important that practically equal amounts of the two solutions should be poured together at the same time, otherwise the proper chemical combination may not take place and the results of the spraying may not be satisfactory.

Ammoniacal Copper Carbonate.—In conspicuous places the Bordeaux mixture is objectionable on account of the deposits of lime and copper that remain on the foliage, and therefore ammoniacal copper carbonate is used. It is a clear, light blue solution which leaves no stain. It is not so adhesive to the foliage as Bordeaux mixture, is washed off with heavy rains, and requires frequent renewals. The formula for making it is as follows:

```
Copper carbonate.....................  5 oz.
Strong ammonia......................  1 qt.
Water to make......................50 gals.
```

Dilute the ammonia with two gallons of water, add enough to the copper carbonate to make a thin paste, pour on about half the ammonia and stir thoroughly. Allow the mixture to settle, and then pour off the top, leaving the undissolved portion behind. Repeat this operation, using small quantities of the remaining ammonia until all the copper sulfate is dissolved, taking no more ammonia than is necessary to complete the solution. Then add the remainder of the required amount of water.

As in the case of insecticides, there are ready-prepared fungicides on the market. These preparations have been steadily improved and are coming into general use. They may cost more than the crude chemicals do when prepared by the user; but they are more economical in the long run, because of the saving of the cost of labor of making them.

SPRAYING APPARATUS

There is now on the market machinery for spraying the smallest bush or the tallest tree. There are atomizers, bucket-pumps, barrel hand-pumps and power-sprayers. What sprayer to get depends upon the work required. No matter what capacity sprayer it is intended to purchase it is always best to communicate with the state experiment station for information and advice. During the last few years rapid strides have been made in the manufacture of spraying apparatus, and it pays to take the trouble to ascertain what is the best on the market.

Bucket-Pumps.—A most serviceable and very cheap apparatus for spraying fruit and medium sized shade-trees is a bucket-pump shown in Plate 42, Fig. 4. When using this sprayer, the insecticide should be mixed in a barrel or other receptacle, and small quantities poured into the bucket from which the mixture is pumped.

Barrel Hand-Pumps.—More powerful than the bucket-pumps are the barrel hand-pumps. These consist of a hand-pump set in a barrel of fifty or sixty gallons capacity which contains the insecticide. They can generally supply from two to four leads of hose and give sufficient pressure to produce a very fine spray. A good hand-pump, mounted on a barrel or tank, furnishes a good outfit for the orchardist and

FLATE 42.—SPRAYERS.

1. Gasoline Power-Sprayer, consisting of an air-cooled cylinder engine directly connected to spray pump, 200-gallon insecticide tank and mechanical agitator operated by the engine. 2. Gasoline Power-Sprayer, consisting of a 115-gallon insecticide tank, 3-horse-power gasoline motor operating a triplex pump. The transmission is by a belt. The agitator is of the jet type. 3. Power-Sprayer operated by liquid carbon dioxid. The liquid gas is in the tube to the left of the 150-gallon insecticide tank. The agitator is of the mechanical type, turned by a crank by the man on

will be found equally satisfactory for spraying shade-trees when only a limited number are to be treated.

Power-Sprayers.—For spraying very large trees and for city work in general, power sprayers are absolutely necessary. There are many kinds of spray outfits of which those run by gasoline and by liquid carbon dioxid are now the most common in use. Gasoline sprayers consist of a gasoline motor, pump, and insecticide tank. The transmission of power from the motor to the pump is either by means of a belt, or the pump and engine are directly connected by reduction gearing. The latter arrangement is much the better. The insecticide tanks are usually of about two hundred gallons capacity.

A very necessary accessory of the insecticide tank is an agitator to stir the spraying mixture while the machine is in operation. This may be either a mechanical contrivance operated by the engine or of the jet type. The latter consists of a jet of the spraying mixture sent back into the tank by the pump. If the capacity of the motor is ample, an agitator of the jet type is excellent; but if the pressure is very much reduced by sending some of the liquid back to the tank, a mechanical agitator is to be preferred.

Whether the agitator be of the jet or the mechanical type, it is very important that it should be worked by the engine and not by man power. When a man is put to turning a crank for eight or ten hours a day, the chances are that the agitator will not work very uniformly. As a result, when such mixtures as arsenate of lead are used, the precipitate will settle and the spraying will be done with clear water. The writer has known of many cases of ineffective spraying work due to inefficient agitating devices.

The sprayers operated by liquid carbon dioxid have

come into general use during the last few years. This type of machine is very easy to operate. The power is supplied by liquid carbon dioxid contained in steel tubes connected with the steel insecticide tank by means of a piece of hose. When the valve of the carbon dioxid container is opened, the liquid in passing through the gas-tube turns into a gas which creates the pressure in the insecticide tank. The amount of the pressure is indicated by a pressure gage. Sufficient force can be supplied by the carbonic-acid gas to spray the tallest trees.

Gas-sprayers are good, but require a supply of gas constantly available, and the actual cost of operation is very expensive. The liquid carbon dioxid costs about a dollar for every one hundred and fifty gallons of insecticide used. On the average, a man sprays about one hundred and fifty gallons of insecticide mixture per day, so that with three nozzles working, the operating cost of gas-sprayers is about three dollars per day. The operating expense of gasoline-sprayers is trifling—only a few cents a day. The simplicity of gas-sprayers, however, makes them frequently desirable even in spite of the additional operating cost. So long as there is a supply of carbon dioxid on hand there is no loss of time during the working day. Gasoline-sprayers sometimes get out of order, and the loss of time for repairs is considerable. If a good mechanic is available to run a gasoline-sprayer there is little loss of time; but a gas-sprayer gives better results in less skilled hands.

The agitator on the gas-sprayers is of the mechanical type, operated by a crank. Care must be taken to see that the man turns the crank every minute of the time that the machine is in operation if a mixture is used that will settle.

Spraying Hose.—The very best hose made is none too

good for spraying work.   It should safely stand a pressure of not less than one hundred and forty pounds to the square inch.   For spraying tall trees it is absolutely necessary to maintain a pressure of about one hundred and twenty pounds. A number of brands of hose now made will answer these requirements.   While it is desirable to use a light hose so that the equipment will be less cumbersome and it will be easier for the workmen to take the lines up the trees, it has been found undesirable to use hose less than one-half inch in diameter.   This is the most common size used, although three-quarter inch and one inch hose are also employed.

Nozzles.—Although the smallest, the nozzle is none the less one of the most important parts of the spraying outfit. It must break up the mixture into the finest particles and send them against the foliage with the greatest possible force.   A very fine, mistlike spray is excellent when the object is simply to cover a large surface; but such a spray has no penetrating power.

The "Vermorel" nozzle, or some modification of it, is now used by almost all makers of spraying machinery.   In this type of nozzle the stream enters a circular chamber tangentially, acquires thereby a rotary motion, and issues from a small, central opening on the upper disk of the chamber. The Vermorel nozzle is especially serviceable in spraying medium sized trees when all the foliage can be easily reached.   This type of nozzle has a disgorging device for forcing out the obstruction when it becomes clogged.

The construction of the "Cyclone" nozzle is similar to that of the Vermorel, and has the same uses; but is not provided with any disgorging device.

The "Bordeaux" nozzle is so constructed that the character of the spray can be changed from a solid stream to a mistlike, fan-shaped spray by turning the handle.

For spraying very large trees, especially elms, the ends of the branches of which are pendulous and impossible for a

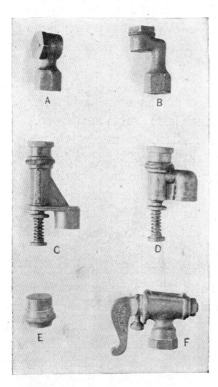

man to reach, nozzles of the jet type are indispensable. Such a nozzle, devised by the writer, is shown in Fig. 30, E. It has a bore of about one-sixteenth of an inch. The mixture comes out in a solid jet; but if there is sufficient pressure, the stream is thrown fifteen feet or more from the nozzle and breaks up finely enough so as to cause the spray to adhere to the foliage.

It is important that as fine a spray as the combination of high pressure and good nozzle will produce should strike the foliage. The finer the spray the better it will adhere to the foliage. A

Fig. 30.—Spray-Nozzles: A and B, types of cyclone nozzles. C and D, types of Vermorel nozzles. E, Jet nozzle. F, Bordeaux nozzle.

coarse spray rolls off the leaf. Especially when spraying with arsenate of lead or other stomach poisons, the efficacy of which depends upon its adhesiveness to the leaves, the use of a fine spray is necessary to secure the best results.

Extension Poles and Spray-Rods.—For reaching the tops of trees bamboo poles are used, which are fastened alongside of the end of the hose.   The nozzle is inserted into the

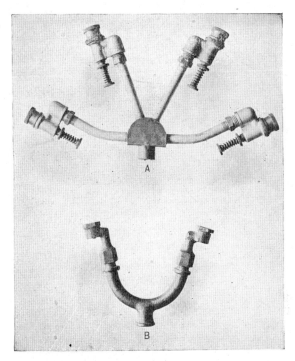

FIG. 31.—Spray "Ys."   A, Four-branched "Y" of Vermorel nozzles. B, Two-branched "Y" of Cyclone nozzles.   These "Ys" may be used in the place of single nozzles.   They cause a more rapid discharge of the spray mixture.

hose, so that the pole serves the purpose of making the spray end of the line rigid.

Spray-rods are now made, however, which make it easier to handle the hose.   The spray-rods consist of aluminum tubes, inside of bamboo poles.   One end of the rod is attached to the hose, the spray mixture passes through the tube and out of the nozzle at the other end.

Precautions in Spraying.—Spraying is one of the most important and expensive operations in the care of trees. To be at all effective it must be very carefully done and cannot be left to ignorant hands. There must be thoroughness in all applications made. The man at the nozzle must know precisely what he is aiming at and how he expects to accomplish his aim. With the best appliances and proper insecticides, failures frequently result if the work is not carefully done.

When applying stomach poisons, the spray should not be continued until the foliage drips too freely, for the effectiveness of the fine mist will then be destroyed. All the globules on the leaf will unite to form a film which will run off and leave little of the poison adhering to it. After a fine mist dries on the leaves, they can be sprayed again and will then hold more poison than would have been possible to apply during one operation.

The application of contact insecticides, however, should be more thorough than that of stomach poisons and continued until the leaves drip. These poisons act only until they dry, and if any insect is not touched it will escape. Stomach poisons adhere to the leaf-tissue, and the chewing insect is bound to get some of the poison if it continues to feed long enough—if not on one part of the leaf then on another.

All spraying mixtures should be carefully strained before being poured into the insecticide tank. This precaution will prevent the clogging of the nozzle.

A warm, sunshiny, calm day is ideal for spraying. When there is no wind there is little waste of spraying material and the insecticide adheres more firmly to the leaves and dries quickly. When doing considerable work, however, that must be finished within a certain time to be effective, one cannot always wait for the ideal day. No spraying, however, should be done on wet days or when rain is anticipated. If it should rain shortly after trees have been sprayed, they should be carefully examined afterward to see if the spraying material has been washed off. If so, the trees should be sprayed again.

CHAPTER X

THE REPAIR AND REPLACING OF TREES

THE REPAIR OF TREES

IF trees were planted and maintained under ideal conditions and were not subject to injuries or diseases they would continue in good condition and health to a very old age. But these conditions are not possible among a community of trees any more than among a community of human beings.

Natural enemies such as windstorms, insect pests, and fungous diseases, failure of placing guards around trees to protect them from horse-bites, the leaving of short stumps in pruning, abrasions caused by overhead wires and general neglect cause serious damage to city trees. Although slight at first such injuries, when left unattended at the time of occurrence, are frequently the first cause of the decay and death of valuable trees.

The preservation of grown trees in a city is sometimes of greater importance than setting out new ones. The repair of trees or tree surgery forms one of the chief and most necessary tasks in the care of shade-trees.

Abrasion of Bark.—One of the simplest cases requiring treatment is a body wound on a tree caused by the abrasion or stripping of the bark. In such cases the thing to do is to cut away with a sharp knife all loose, ragged, or injured bark as far as the injury extends. Bark once loosened can never attach itself to the trunk again. When left on the tree it soon dries and decays and forms a shelter for insects and fungus spores. After the injured bark has been carefully removed, the exposed wood should be painted with coal-tar to prevent the checking of the exposed wood. A callus will soon form and in time the entire scar will heal.

Bridge-Grafting. — When the abrasion of the bark extends almost around the tree, or if a tree is completely girdled, a connection between the separate parts of the trunk may be reestablished by bridge-grafting. (Fig. 32.) The edges of the girdle are trimmed, and cions are inserted under the bark so as to bridge the wound. These cions are cut to a wedge shape on either end and are inserted between the bark and the wood. A cloth bandage is tied about each edge of the wound to hold the bark in place over the cions. Melted grafting wax is then poured or molded over the entire work, so as to cover the exposed

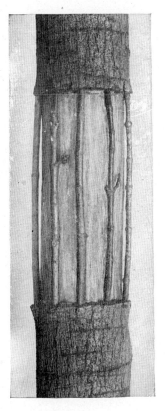

Fig. 32.—Method of bridge-grafting a girdled trunk.

wood and also the edges of the bark for two or three inches from the wound.

Grafting wax may be made as follows:

Resin.................................4 parts
Beeswax...............................2 parts
Tallow ....1 part

Melt in mass, pour into a tub or pail of cold water, then work with greased hands until it develops a grain and becomes the color of taffy candy.

If instead of one part tallow, one and a half parts of linseed-oil are used, and the ingredients then melted, the grafting wax can be drawn out for use without any necessity of remelting. The hands should be greased when working the wax.

Breakages in Storms.—When a limb breaks in a storm the fracture is usually very rough and some of the bark is stripped. The branch should be cut back close to a crotch and the scar painted with coal-tar, just as in pruning. Any loose bark must be removed.

Filling of Cavities.—The mutilation of trees by horses has already been discussed. Any neglected injury to a tree in which the bark is stripped from the trunk, causes the wood to rot and the decay is carried to the centre of the tree. Frequently such cavities can be treated and the life of the tree greatly prolonged.

The repair of tree cavities is very much like the process of filling a tooth. All decayed and diseased wood is removed as far as the living tissue. (Plate 43.) A great variety of tools is found useful in this process of scooping out the bad wood: a ship bit, chisel and hammer, gouge, adze and hatchet can be employed. It is found that in old cavities, the bark, in an effort to cover up the wound, is deposited in thick rolls around the edges that turn inwardly. It is necessary to remove all this tissue to such parts of the trunk that belong to the natural contour of the tree, to the points AA, Fig. 33.

Every cavity requires different methods of procedure in the way it is cleaned, in the amount removed and the means

PLATE 43.—FILLING A LARGE CAVITY OF AN ELM-TREE.

1. On the outside the injury does not seem serious. When the probing begins, 2 and 3, it is found that the decay extends far into the tree. Many kinds of tools are used to clean the wound. 4. The cavity ready for filling. 5. An idea of the size of the cavity. 6. The tree restored.

employed for the reenforcement of the tree or the retention
of the filling. The cavity is finished in a way that it will
retain the filling. In the case of small ones it is sufficient if
the interiors are made larger than the openings. Shallow
cavities and those of considerable size are treated in another

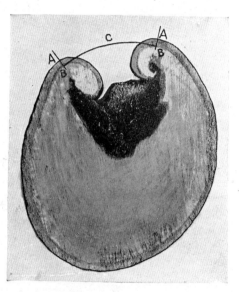

FIG. 33.—A transverse section of a tree showing the precautions to be
taken when preparing a cavity for filling. The rolls of tissue must be
cut away to the points A A, and all decayed wood removed. The
filling must follow the natural contour of the tree, B C B, and stop at
the points B B, depressed a distance equal to the thickness of the bark.

way. A deep channel is cut just inside of the opening, all
around the periphery, and this helps to retain the cement.
Before filling, the cavity is sterilized by washing with an
antiseptic solution of copper sulfate, one pound to fifteen
gallons of water, and then covered with molten coal-tar. In
order to secure a better adhesion of the cement to the walls
of the cavity, the hole is filled before the tar hardens. To

insure the firmer retention of the filling in the tree the cavities are studded with nails. When a tree is weak because of a large cavity, steel braces are sometimes inserted horizontally and vertically for reenforcement.

Small cavities are filled with a mixture of two parts of sand to one part of Portland cement. Larger openings, several cubic feet in volume, are filled by using broken stone and brick with the concrete. In this way it is easier to build up the filling, and its strengthening power is increased. After the filling has had time to stiffen, but not to become perfectly hard, it is finished with cement, a trowel being used to shape it according to the contour of the tree.

An extremely important point to remember is that the filling must not be brought up flush with the outside of the bark of the tree; but must stop at a depth equal to the thickness of the bark and the filling shaped to follow the contour of the tree, as shown by the line B C B, Fig. 33. This precaution must be taken to enable the healing callus to overgrow the filling. If not very large, the tissue may in time completely heal over the cement and bury it, just the same as the stub left when a limb is removed. (Plate 44, Fig. 3.)

It is a good plan, when the cavity is ready for filling, to cut a strip of bark about one-half inch wide all the way around the periphery of the opening, as shown in Plate 44, Fig. 4. The cement can be brought up flush with the wood. The healing callus will start to roll over the wood (Plate 44, Fig. 5), and then over the cement, hermetically sealing the cavity. The edges of the wound only, or the surface of the entire filling may be painted or covered with coal-tar.

When the hollow trunks of trees are filled with concrete, they are immensely strengthened and are not in danger of

PLATE 44.—EXAMPLES OF TREE-SURGERY.

1. Cavity in a tree cleaned ready for a coating of coal-tar and filling. 2. The cavity filled, showing the cement depressed a distance equal to the thickness of the bark. 3. The same tree three years later, callus overgrowing filling. 4. Before the filling was done in this example, a narrow strip of bark was cut around the periphery of the opening and the filling then brought up flush with the wood. 5. The same a year later. The healing callus is beginning to roll over the wood. 6. Injury caused by banding a crotch. 7. Large knot-hole in trunk of white maple, showing ring of tissue around opening. 8. Side view of the same. A cut is made along the line A B. 9. The decayed wood is removed and cavity filled flush with saw-cut. Callus is beginning to overgrow the wound.

being overthrown by strong winds as trees of which the trunks are hollow shells. The concrete acts as a pillar which reenforces the tree.

Knot-Holes.—Equally as serious and more numerous than

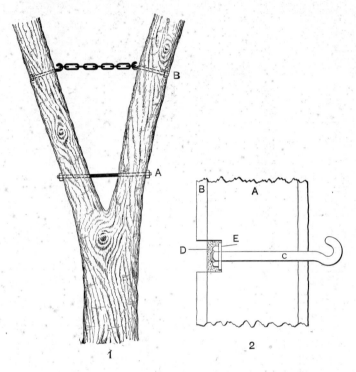

FIG. 34.—1. Methods of strengthening a weak crotch: A, by means of a bolt. B, by means of hook-bolts and chain.   2. Vertical section of branch, showing method of bolting. A, Wood. B, Bark. C, Bolt. D, Cement. E, Washer and nut. Healing tissue will overcap the cement.

wounds on trunks of trees are knot-holes caused by the decay of stumps left by improper pruning. In these cases the grain of the wood running toward the centre of the tree instead of vertically, the decay is more easily carried to the

heart. When the stump is left the new tissue makes an
effort to overgrow the stub, so to speak, and the result is
that a thick layer of wood is deposited at the base of the
crotch. (Plate 26, Fig. 3.) When the stub rots and falls
out, this tissue remains like a ring around the opening of
the knot-hole. (Plate 44, Fig. 7.) To fill such a cavity
properly, it is generally best to make a cut across this ring
close to the trunk, A B, Plate 44, Fig. 8, then scrape out
all the decayed wood and fill the cavity flush with the saw
cut. Although by this means the area of the scar is increased it is brought in more intimate contact with the
healing callus and will be like a cut of an amputated
branch. The callus will form over the wood first (Plate 44,
Fig. 9), and then over the cement and bury it.

Cavities resulting from other causes, such as those made
by borers, can be treated the same way. Surface wounds
need only a painting with coal-tar; but if the decay is deep
it needs scraping and filling with cement.

Crotches.—It frequently happens that a tree forms a
sharp angle by the division, near the ground, into two or
three limbs. The addition of the annual layers of wood and
the swaying of the tree cause a prying apart of the limbs
at this point, and in time a split is the result. It is then
necessary to brace the crotch to prevent the branches from
breaking off.

A common though wrong method of repairing such a
defect in a tree has been to put a band around the two limbs
forming the fork. The result of such a method is shown in
Plate 44, Fig. 6. The action of the band around one-half
of the circumference of the tree has resulted in partly girdling it. It has cut into the layers of new growth and the
tree has been disfigured. The proper way to brace a crotch

is to run a bolt through the branches, as shown in Fig. 34, by boring holes through them. With the growth of the tree, the nuts holding the bolt are buried by new tissue and no injury results to the tree.

A great many trees can be saved by the practise of tree surgery and their life prolonged for a great many years. It is, however, work that requires great judgment and skill, as every tree presents a different problem and one should not entrust his trees for treatment to impostors who claim to possess miraculous means of curing trees of all diseases.

MAINTENANCE OF UNIFORMITY

It is very disagreeable to see among a line of street-trees one or two failing specimens, more so than among a group of trees, or trees scattered over a large area. The task of maintaining all the trees on a long street in a uniformly good state is sometimes a difficult one, because of varying conditions of soil and other factors. Frequently the trees on a low portion of a street will not be so thrifty as those higher up because the drainage is poorer and the water-table close to the roots. In order to maintain in the same state of health all the trees of a street plantation, some specimens may need extra culture, watering, and fertilizing to enable them to keep pace with their more vigorous neighbors.

PARTIAL REPLACING

When specimens are drooping or sickly and do not respond to culture; or when they are hopelessly injured in some way, so that they cannot be restored, they should be replaced with new trees. The new trees should be of the same species and, if possible, of the same size as the trees which constitute the plantation of which they are to form a part. For this purpose a nursery has to be maintained where trees of different species and sizes are grown, ready to take the place of trees that fail.

The method outlined above is followed in Paris. The trees that are to be trained for transplanting, to take the place of large specimens, are set out in the municipal nursery about twenty feet apart each way to allow room for development. The branching is gradually raised and then fixed at the proper height. Every three or four years the roots are cut or circumscribed so that they do not spread out, but are made to grow compactly, restricted within a certain volume. This work of cutting the roots consists of digging a circular ditch around the base of the tree and cutting the roots as neatly as possible. The size of the ditch depends upon the size of the tree. Thus in the case of a tree about four inches in diameter, three feet from the base, the circular ditch is about three feet in diameter and about two and one-half feet deep. After the roots have been cut the soil is replaced and closely packed.

In the cases of trees that have been trained as described above, the Board of Works of Paris prescribes the dimensions of the ball of earth and roots with which trees of different sizes are to be transplanted about as follows:

Diameter of Tree Three Feet from the Base.	Diameter of Ball of Earth.	Depth.
3 in. to 5 in.	3 ft. to 3 ft. 3 in.	2 ft.
5¼ in. to 8 in.	3 ft. 4 in. to 3 ft. 10 in.	2 ft. 6 in.
8¼ in. to 12 in.	4 ft. to 5 ft.	3 ft.
12¼ in. to 14 in.	5 ft. 10 in. to 6 ft. 4 in.	3 ft. 4 in.
14¼ in. to 18 in.	7 ft. 6 in. to 8 ft. 2 in.	4 ft.

Transplanting of this kind is usually done in late fall and winter. The specimens are carried in heavy trucks especially constructed for the purpose of moving large trees.

RENEWAL OF PLANTATIONS

As the trees on a street advance in age and the failing specimens become in the majority, the plantations would look ragged if an attempt were made to replace only the dead trees while those that were still alive, but also on the verge of decay, were left standing. Then when the new trees reestablished themselves, the old trees would die, and under such conditions it would no longer be possible to maintain a uniform planting. It is best to set out new trees entirely. The soil should be renewed and as a general practise it is best to replant with a different species.

Dr. W. A. Murrill writes in his bulletin on "Shade-Trees,"[1] "I was struck by the absence of old or even large trees on the streets of Paris. All trees seem about the same in age and size, and all are in the very prime of life."

The splendid condition and the imposing effect of the street-trees of Paris is due to the most painstaking methods of planting and culture; the partial replacing of failing specimens just so long as the uniformity of the trees can be so maintained; and, finally, the renewal of the plantations entirely when the majority of the trees begin to fail.

The planting of small trees between old ones is a bad practise, because it is hard to establish young specimens in such cases. They grow slowly on account of the cutting off of sunlight, they tend to shoot upward rather than to spread, and the roots of the old trees invade upon the available food

[1] "Shade-Trees," by W. A. Murrill, Bulletin 205, Cornell University Agricultural Experiment Station.

of the young trees. If, however, it is found desirable to interplant young trees among large ones, which are to be removed when the young trees grow up, then the branches of the old trees should be so trimmed as to allow plenty of sunlight to reach the small ones, and the roots of the neighboring trees should be cut so that they will not interfere with the new specimens.

The period of the duration of life of city trees is much less than that of the same species growing in the forest. Their length of life depends upon the conditions of soil and the care and culture bestowed upon them.

CHAPTER XI

WHO SHALL PLANT AND CARE FOR STREET-TREES

In every town and city of the country where trees are most abundant and where they are most likely to thrive, at one time or other there arises the problem of taking care of those trees and of setting out new ones. There comes a time when a certain species of tree is attacked by an insect, when the trees along a certain street need pruning, when trees are to be guarded from horse-bites and passing vehicles; or when it is desirable to plant a newly opened street.

INDIVIDUAL PLANTING

There are two ways by which the work of planting and caring for street-trees can be accomplished. The work must be done either by individual land owners or public officials. The prevailing policy of most of our cities has been to leave this task to the individuals who own the property on a certain street. The results thus obtained have been very unsatisfactory. It will be an easy matter for those at all concerned with municipal improvements to picture to themselves a street or a number of streets in any city where the plan of the individual control of street-trees exists.

What picture do these streets present? There are long stretches that are not planted at all. The trees that have been set out bear evidence of the diversity of taste of the planters. There are half a dozen or more species of trees on

231

the same street, undesirable mixed with desirable, of all shapes and sizes, set either too closely or too far apart. In some cases the trees are not trimmed at all and the limbs are so low as to touch the heads of pedestrians; in others they are pruned too high. The trees have been left unprotected by guards, many of them have been bitten by horses, and there is evidence that they have been injured by destructive pests. The writer has had the opportunity of studying the street-trees of a great many towns and cities in different parts of the country and the conditions described above are universal.

Especially in the control of insects which infest certain species of trees from time to time the system, or rather the lack of system, of the individual care of street-trees utterly fails. The citizen is entirely powerless to accomplish anything. He may plant an undesirable species of tree if the task is left to him, but in insect fighting he will do even less. His efforts will come to naught if his neighbor allows the pest to remain on *his* trees. In the extermination of insects in a city it is absolutely necessary that all the infested trees be treated in order to obtain effective results. It is impossible to have concerted action on the part of thousands of people of a community in the treatment of infested trees at the same time. Insect fighting requires persistence and knowledge of what to do at the proper time to obtain results. There is a period in the life history of most of our tree pests when it may be most easily destroyed. This stage is not always at the time when the most injury is apparent, or when the average citizen wakes up to the necessity of doing something. The life history of the pests must be known in order that treatment may be given at the right time. Besides, to spray trees of considerable size requires an apparatus which the average citizen cannot be expected to have.

The injury to trees by borers is a case in point. The foliage does not show the effects of the damage nor do the limbs begin to die until three or four years after the caterpillars of the borers do their fatal work. Then the people wonder why the trees are dying. Hundreds of sugar maples died in the northern section of the State of New Jersey during the years of 1905 and 1906 as a result of the ravages of the borers a few years before that time. Attention to them at the time the insects were active would have saved the trees.

We cannot blame the individual for unsatisfactory results. We are seeking in the planting of shade-trees that which is for the common good of all, and we expect the work to be done by the citizens without instruction, without system, and leave to each one, if it so pleases him, to do his share when and how he desires. It is the system that is wrong, and the remedy can readily suggest itself. Other municipal interests are vested in commissions, committees, or other organized bodies. Experience has shown that in order to obtain the greatest degree of excellence in the planting and care of street-trees, the matter must be entrusted to a similar body, and a shade-tree department should be incorporated in every municipality.

MUNICIPAL CONTROL

It is only when the planting and care of street-trees is vested in a special department that all the principles essential to secure the most stately and impressive effect of highway planting can be applied; such as the choice of the proper species, the use of one variety on a street, setting out of specimens at uniform and proper distances apart, and the protection and cultivation of the trees afterward. The task of such a department is not a mean one in the life of the modern city. In the prospectus issued by the New Orleans Parking Commission, created in 1909, to have exclusive control of the planting and care of street-trees in that city, the Commission beautifully defines its function and its mission as follows:

"If this Commission diligently searches out its true relationships in the beautiful or fine arts, where it rightfully belongs, and studiously possesses itself of that largeness of thought and trained facility of imagination, inspiring within itself the idealizing faculty, whereby the true architect and painter project visually the creations of genius before work is laid on drawing board or brush on canvas, then, of very necessity, as like begets like, there will begin throughout this city a development in pure art, dignified in orderly elegance and grace, beautiful in unity, becoming more apparent and impressive with each succeeding year, just as the Washington city of to-day was visually projected as a living painting by l'Enfant a hundred years ago—and the city of Cleveland, with its newly projected grandeur by the Chapter of the American Institute of Architects.

"To initiate this is the work we are called upon to do—a work that must be carefully mapped according to specifications in the general plan, in which every tree planted and dollar spent shall count just that much toward the end in view; which is the real and practical uplifting and betterment of the whole community—physically, mentally, morally, in the actual comfort and pleasure of living and in a growing sense of self-regard and civic pride. It is a home mission work in a strictly rational, business way, with certainty of returns, far exceeding expenditure; an enterprise rich in utility; not of a mechanical or directly commercial kind; for the city does not propose to open a wood yard or grow trees for lumber; but it does contemplate something far more useful in a beautifully environed, clean, wholesome, contented citizenship; for as the environment, so are the people. If the one is slovenly and degraded, so is the other; and the contrary is true, as proved in every community; particularly in large manufacturing centres where the extremes of comparison are so distressingly in contrast."

Washington.—While the idea of the municipal control of street-trees is not new, it is only during the last decade that the benefits derived from such a system have become generally recognized. In this country the City of Washington offers the most mature results of the system of public control of street-trees.

The department for the planting and care of trees is officially known as the Trees and Parkings Division of the District of Columbia, and was first organized in the year 1872. At the close of the year 1909, there were 94,799 trees along the streets, all of which were planted under municipal control and paid for by the city. An average of eighty men is employed by the department during the working seasons. The annual appropriation for maintenance of the shade-trees of Washington is usually $40,000. This amount is half of what is appropriated in Paris for the care of fewer trees, and strong efforts are made each year for a substantial increase in this amount, it being felt that at least double the sum could be used with advantage.

Paris.—The street-trees of Paris are under public control. The plantations on the public highways number about 86,000 trees. In this figure are not included the specimens in the

squares, gardens, and parks. The annual expenses of maintenance are about $80,000. This sum is spent on wages
of workmen, repairs of guards, grills, etc.; the supply of
new soil to drooping specimens and the replacing of dead
trees. The work is done by a force of one hundred and two
men, divided into gangs entrusted with a certain kind of
work, such as planting, transplanting, pruning, etc. The
work of transplanting large trees in trucks is done by special
contractors. The trees existing on the public highways are
planted and cared for at the expense of the city. The Prefect of the Department of the Seine writes that about eighteen hundred trees are planted annually to take the place of
dead trees. New streets are also planted, but these plantations are very small, as trees have already been set out on
all the streets that are sufficiently wide to have them.

New York and Other Cities.—By an act of the year 1902,
of the Laws of the State of New York, the jurisdiction of
the Park Boards of Greater New York was extended to the
preservation and planting of trees on the streets of the several boroughs. Among the other cities of the country that
have assumed control of the street-trees within recent years
are Chicago, St. Louis, Cleveland, Buffalo, Hartford, New
Orleans, and Pittsburgh. Through the efforts of local improvement societies of a great many towns and cities of the
country efforts are being made to provide in some way for
the proper planting and maintenance of highway trees.

States.—The States that have passed the most advanced
laws along lines of securing the more general adoption of
the system of the municipal control of street-trees are New
Jersey, Massachusetts, and Pennsylvania. New Jersey has
been the pioneer State of the Union in the enactment of a
model statute in 1893, to provide for the planting and care

PLATE 45.—STREET-PLANTING BY MUNICIPAL TREE DEPARTMENT.

Hilton Street, East Orange, N. J., Planted with Oriental Planes by the Shade-Tree Commission in April, 1906.
View was taken in August, 1909.

of shade-trees on the highways of the municipalities of the State. Massachusetts, in 1899, passed an act providing that every town must elect a tree warden, and defined the duties and powers of the office. In 1907, Pennsylvania passed a shade-tree law, modeled after the New Jersey Act of 1893 and its amendments. The texts of these model laws are given in Chapter XIII.

New Jersey and Pennsylvania.—The laws of New Jersey and Pennsylvania which provide for the establishment of shade-tree commissions are not of general application to all municipalities, but are of local option. They become operative in a town or city only after its adoption by the town or city council. Up to date, thirty-one towns and cities in New Jersey have established shade-tree commissions. These are Allendale, Arlington, Bloomfield, Caldwell, Camden, Chatham, East Orange, East Rutherford, Elizabeth, Jersey City, Kearny, Madison, Metuchen, Montclair, Morristown, Newark, New Brunswick, Nutley, Passaic, Perth Amboy, Plainfield, Point Pleasant, Rahway, Ridgefield, Ridgewood, Roselle, Rutherford, South Orange, Summit, Westfield and Woodbury. The Pennsylvania statute has been adopted by Ambridge, Pittsburgh, and Wilkes-Barre.

The New Jersey act of 1893 was amended in the years of 1905 and 1906. The law of Pennsylvania of 1907 combines the act of 1893 of New Jersey and its amendments. Briefly, the provisions of these acts may be summarized as follows:

When by resolution of the city council it is decided that the law shall become operative in a city, then from that time all matters pertaining to shade-trees are placed in the hands of the respective commissions. All work is carried on in a systematic way and the trees are planted, pruned, sprayed, and removed under the direction of the commissioners. Wherein these commissions differ from other similar bodies is that they have the power of initiative in the matter of planting. They decide that a certain street is to be planted and determine the species of tree. An advertisement of the intention to plant is inserted for two weeks in the public newspapers, and all persons interested in the improvement are given an opportunity to be heard. After the work is done the commissioners meet and certify a list to the receiver of taxes on which are given the names of the owners in front of whose property trees were set out and the cost of the work. These assessments are entered by the receiver of taxes on the annual tax bill and are paid the same way as any other legal lien. The cost of pruning, spraying, removing dead trees and repairing old ones is provided for by a general appropriation.

These laws give the shade-tree commissions the power to pass ordinances for the planting, protection, regulation, and control of street-trees. These ordinances have been extremely efficient in securing the protection of trees. They do away entirely with the abuses of public utilities corporations who in the past have so ruthlessly mutilated and destroyed trees along highways for the passage of overhead wires. In fact some of the most important work of a shade-tree commission is to protect the trees already existing in a city.

Massachusetts.—The laws of Massachusetts in regard to the planting and care of shade-trees in towns and cities are among the most progressive in the country. The "Tree Warden Act" of 1899, provided that every town must elect a tree warden, and defined the duties and powers of the office. This act did not apply to cities; but by the laws of

1910, the "Tree Warden Act" has been extended in practically all its provisions, except that requiring the election of a tree warden, to the cities of the commonwealth as well. Thus the act of 1899 of Massachusetts and its amendments secure the regulation of the planting and care of shade-trees in practically every town and city of the State.

The charters of the Massachusetts cities vary so widely in the provisions for local government that it was not possible to secure uniformity in the election or appointment of shade-tree officials or in the matter of administration. Consequently, each city is free to appoint under its special charter provision, some board or officer for the care of public shade-trees.

There are now 301 towns and 33 cities in Massachusetts. Every town at its annual election elects a tree warden. Every city but one has made provision of some kind for the care of the shade-trees, either by the appointment of a special officer, or by giving authority to an already existing officer or board, as follows:

Officer or Board	Number of Cities
Park Commission	8
City Improvement Committee	1
City Forester	3
Tree and Forest Warden	1
Tree Warden	1
Forest Commissioner	1
Board of Public Works	5
Commission of Public Works	2
Street Commissioner	2
Board of Street Commissioners	2
Superintendent of Streets	4
Superintendent of Highways	1
City Engineer	1

PRINCIPLES UNDERLYING SHADE-TREE LEGISLATION

When a department for the planting and care of street-trees is established in a city, there frequently arises misunderstandings with the property-owners regarding the relation which the shade-tree has to the street. The placing of shade-trees under municipal control is of comparatively recent introduction, and therefore, although the citizen is accustomed to regulations affecting the pavements and the sidewalks, he still considers the shade-tree as something affecting only his own house and not as something contributing to the value of the entire street.

For example, a man is used to paying assessments for the paving of the roadway, for the curbing and the laying of the sidewalk, and still he does not absolutely own the pavement. He cannot open up the street without good reason, and unless he has permission from the city authorities to do so. He cannot take up the macadam pavement and replace it with asphalt if it so pleases him. It is an accepted fact that as regards the paving of the highway there must be a uniformity of plan that will be productive of the best results for the benefit of every resident of the street.

The relation of the shade-tree to the highway is the same as that of any other road improvement. The tree is something which benefits not only the abutting property-owner but the entire street, and it is upon this idea that all legislation regarding the planting and care of shade-trees is based. A man may plant a shade-tree along the street-line, but he does not own it in the sense that he owns the trees within the property-line. Neither he nor anybody else has the right to mutilate or cut down the street-tree, for the whole street would incur a loss by such action.

One of the sections of the ordinance passed by the East Orange Shade-Tree Commission provides that no tree shall be planted in any of the public highways until such tree shall have been first approved and the place where it is to be planted designated by the Shade-Tree Commission and a permit granted therefor. If the citizen were permitted to plant shade-trees as he saw fit he might plant a tree unsuited for street use or might place it close to a tree on his neighbor's property, and in either case would produce a result detrimental to the street. The other sections of the ordinance relating to the protection of trees also embody this idea, that the shade-tree is something in which all the residents of the street share.

The Supreme Court of the State of Illinois, in the case of Baker *vs.* the Town of Normal, in Laws of Illinois, volume 81, page 109, says:—"The town under its charter has the control of streets, may improve them and adorn them. It may permit its citizens to improve and adorn that part of the street in front of his lot, but the improvement and adornment does not thereby become the property of the citizen. The planting of a shade-tree in the street by a citizen by permission of the village or city authorities is a gratuity to the public, and the citizen has no more right to control the shade-tree so planted than he would have had it been planted by the city authorities. The control is in the public. The adjoining proprietor has a common interest with other citizens in these shade-trees and incidentally derives a special benefit from their existence, but no title of authority over them, as against the public."

A little over two years ago, two citizens came into my office and complained that one of the residents of their street had cut down a tree in front of his own house. They were

greatly agitated about the matter and told me that the removal of the tree was something in which every property
owner was concerned, as the resulting gap spoiled the uniformity of the row of the remaining trees. I investigated
the matter and found that a tree had indeed been removed,
but that permission had been previously obtained from our
office. The tree in question was in a diseased and dangerous condition, could not be saved, and it was the advice of
our office to remove the tree and put a new one in its place.
When the complainants were informed why the tree was
removed, they felt satisfied that their interests had been
protected. Their action in bringing complaint when they
thought that the tree had been unwarrantably cut down was
a just one, and it illustrates the point that the destruction of
a shade-tree is something that affects the entire street.

During the winter of 1909, I was called to Harrisburg to
help in the movement to organize a department that would
look after the shade-trees of that city. One of the citizens
told me that he was going along a street one day when he
saw a man cutting off the branches of a large tree in front of
his place and leaving nothing but the trunk. He asked him
why he was spoiling the tree and the man replied: "I can
make use of the wood, and don't care for the shade." As
there were no regulations in that city in regard to shade-
trees, that man, in spite of the protestations of his neighbors,
went on with his work and left the mutilated specimen as a
permanent eyesore to the residents of the street.

CHAPTER XII

A DEPARTMENT OF MUNICIPAL ARBORICULTURE

No matter by what legislative provision a town or city establishes a shade-tree department, its task after organization should be the same, namely: to secure the very best results obtainable in street decoration for the benefit of the whole city, according to the most approved scientific principles and methods. The laws of Massachusetts provide for the appointment of tree wardens in towns. The statutes of New Jersey and Pennsylvania provide for the establishment of commissions to have the control of trees along public highways. As practically operated the commissioners serve as an organization, and they employ a trained arboriculturist who has charge of the executive work.

OFFICIAL IN CHARGE OF STREET-TREES

To secure the best results there must be one official to carry out the duties which a shade-tree department demands. Those in charge of city trees have been variously designated as "Tree Wardens," "Tree Doctors," and City Foresters." The writer has always felt that to call one charged with the preservation and care of shade-trees a "forester" is a wrong application of that word. He agrees with Dr. Fernow[1] that the term "Tree Warden" is a more expressive title for such an official. The term "Arboriculturist" is also a very apt one. A forester is concerned with

[1] "The Care of Trees," by Bernhard E. Fernow.

the economic side of tree growth, the product of the tree: its wood. The arboriculturist cultivates trees for their esthetic value and their shade, and deals with them only in their living state. To call one in charge of tree culture in a city a "city forester" is to imply that the city is growing trees for lumber. The propagation of trees in cities has an entirely different aim, and trees cultivated along streets become by their beauty and utility more valuable than the lumber which they contain. When a tree is cut down it is no longer of value to the street nor does it interest the arboriculturist. Perhaps a better term than "Tree Warden" or "Municipal Arboriculturist" will be invented that will express adequately the functions of an official in charge of the planting and care of city trees.

The tree warden who understands his position correctly has a greater task to perform than simply the propagation of trees according to scientific principles. He must be an enthusiast in his work and inspire among the people of a community the proper appreciation of the value of trees. The people will then in turn help him in the administration of his office; for his success will largely depend upon the interest of the people of his town or city in their trees and the support which they give him. He must also appreciate the responsibility of his position as the guardian of one of the chief resources for maintaining the beauty and health of a city.

TREE CENSUS

In its details, the work of the tree warden is partly that of the municipal engineer. It is necessary to enumerate the existing trees, to make layouts for new plantations and keep records of these. In order to care intelligently for his charges the municipal arboriculturist must know how many trees come under his jurisdiction.   One of the first things he should do when he assumes the task of caring for the trees of a city is the taking of a tree census: that is, the enumeration of all the trees of the city in field books and the careful plotting of these trees on maps prepared for that purpose.

Field Books.—A form of field book for the enumeration of street-trees designed by the writer has proved very adequate and could be used advantageously in any town or city. The book is made in a form similar to an engineer's transit or level field book.   A few leaves from such a book are inserted after page 275. The size of the leaves is four and one-half inches by eight inches.   The right hand page is cross-sectioned into fifths of inches.   On these pages each street is plotted to a scale of fifty feet to the inch.   Four red lines drawn vertically in the centre of the page represent in conventional form the sidewalks of the street of which the trees are to be recorded.   The inner two lines are the curb-lines, and the outer two are the property-lines.   The divisions of the abutting properties are indicated by lines drawn at right angles to the outer red lines.   The cross streets are similarly indicated by lines making the proper angles with the curb and the property lines.   This field book admits of the plotting of sections of street 350 feet in length on each page.

On the leaves from the field book inserted after page 275 is plotted the short street, "Shepard Street," a map of which is shown, Fig. 35.   The cross-sectioned paper obviates using a scale in transferring the street to the field book. Likewise in the indication of the position of the trees, the cross-sectioning will be a guide, as the sides of the little squares represent ten feet.

On the left hand page are given the descriptions of the trees.   At the top of the page the name of the street and the date are noted. The columns are headed as "Tree Number," "Species," "Diameter," "Condition," and "Remarks." Beginning at one end of the street, corner of Beech Street, the first tree is numbered as one. Its distance from the corner is found to be fourteen feet. The tree is shown by a small black circle on the right hand page. The small "c" after "14'" indicates that the distance is from the corner. The tree is then described on the left hand page. It is a Norway maple, five inches in diameter, measured breast high, and in good condition. In the column under "Remarks" is entered anything about the condition of the trees that is abnormal or unusual.

The distance between the first and second trees is then measured, noted on the right hand page and the entry of the tree made on the left hand page. And so on the enumeration continues, first on one side of the street and then on the other. To do this work effectively and rapidly, three men are required in the gang: a rear chainman, a head chainman, and a man who makes the entry of the trees. Distances are measured from the centre of one tree to the centre of another. The head chainman calls off the distances and the enumerator notes all of the other data which are entered on the left hand page.

The method of rating trees with respect to their condition depends upon the object sought in enumerating them. So many factors are to be considered in the judgment of the condition of a tree that it would be impossible in taking a general census to enter a detailed description of each tree. A general method of classification therefore has to be adopted that will enable the tree warden, from a study of the records, to form a good idea of the general condition of the trees on a street.

In judging the condition of a tree, its immediate future rather than its present state should be considered. It is suggested that trees may be rated as "good," "medium," and "bad." A tree is rated "good" that is in full vigor and gives no indication of immediate decline. A tree is called "medium" which begins to decline, but which can be restored to vigor by culture, fertilization, pruning, treatment of cavities, or in some other way. A tree is "bad," which is in such a state of decline that it cannot be restored to vigor.

A summary of a survey of trees in a city may be exemplified by the following:

SUMMARY OF SURVEY OF STREET-TREES IN EAST ORANGE, PLANTED BEFORE THE SHADE-TREE COMMISSION WAS ESTABLISHED

Species.	Number.	Species.	Number.
Ailantus	6	Maple, Norway	1,210
Apple	1	Maple, Red	2,847
Arborvitæ	1	Maple, Silver	2,228
Ash, White	81	Maple, Sugar	2,232
Aspen, Large-toothed	1	Maple, Sycamore	51
Beech, American	6	Mulberry, White	1
Buckeye	7	Oak, Pin	23
Catalpa	30	Oak, Red	11
Cherry, Cultivated	2	Oak, Swamp white	11
Cherry, Wild	4	Oak, White	19
Dogwood, Flowering	3	Pine, White	5
Elm, American	995	Poplar, Carolina	728
Elm, Slippery	2	Poplar, Lombardy	2
Gum, Sour	1	Poplar, White	7
Gum, Sweet	5	Plane, American	22
Hickory, Mockernut	2	Plane, Oriental	6
Hickory, Pignut	6	Sassafras	2
Hickory, Shagbark	2	Silverbell	1
Hornbeam	4	Spruce, Norway	2
Horse-chestnut	177	Tulip	9
Linden, American	133	Walnut, Black	2
Linden, European	46	Walnut, White	1
Locust, Honey	1	Willow, Weeping	4
Maple, Ash-leaved	13	Total	10,953

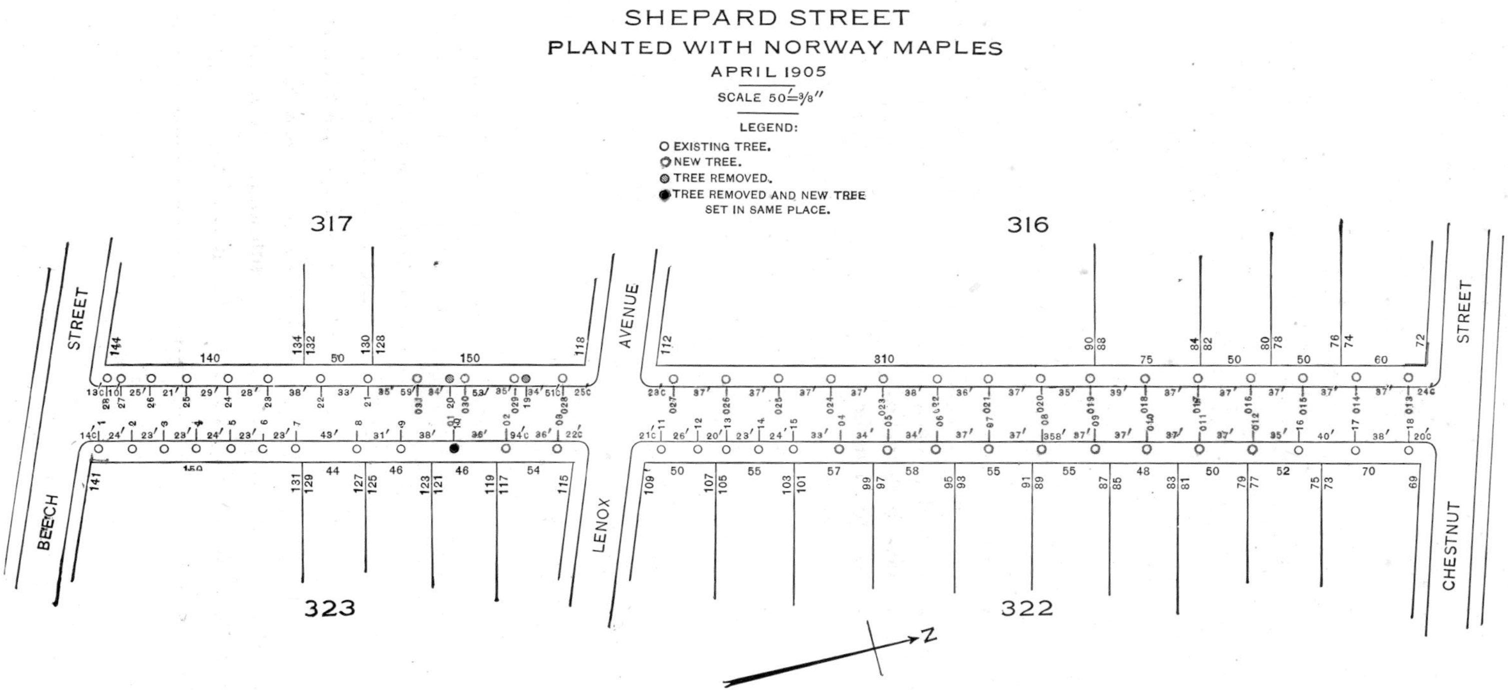

Fig. 35.—Showing method of plotting street-trees. This figure is drawn to a scale of fifty feet to three-eighths of an inch. The original office maps, however, are drawn to a scale of fifty feet to one inch. Sheets of paper, 24 x 12 inches in size, are convenient for these maps, the street being continued on as many sheets as its length demands.

As regards the condition of the trees, they have been rated as good, medium, and bad, as follows:

Condition.	Number.
Good	9,422
Medium	558
Bad	973
Total	10,953

The sizes of the trees, measured breast high, are as follows:

Size.	Number.
Under 6 inches	1,698
6 inches to 12 inches	3,089
13 inches to 18 inches	3,947
19 inches to 24 inches	1,451
Over 24 inches	768
Total	10,953

Mapping the Trees.—The method of plotting the trees to scale on maps is shown in Fig. 35. This figure is drawn to a scale of fifty feet to three-eighths of an inch, to accommodate it on a page of this book. The original office maps, however, are carefully drawn to a scale of fifty feet to the inch, and on them are shown the width of the street from property-line to property-line, the width of the sidewalks, the frontage of the abutting properties, the city block map, and the lot numbers. The divisions of the abutting properties are likely to change when sales and transfers are made. It is therefore best to indicate in lead pencil the lines marking the property divisions, and the figures showing the widths of the properties and the lot numbers. The trees noted in the field book are then drawn on the map. A good conventional form for existing trees is a small black circle.

The spacing of the trees and the numbers given them are also indicated.

Value of Tree Census.—The maps are found to be extremely valuable office records in a great many ways. When a request is made for attention to a certain tree on a street, the tree warden can immediately find out the species and condition of the tree by referring to his field book and maps. When it is proposed to plant certain streets which have some existing trees, the records can be used to determine the trees that are to be removed, and adequate provision made for the planting of new ones.

Records of street-trees are invaluable in organizing a campaign against an insect pest attacking a certain species. By knowing the number and distribution of affected trees coming under his jurisdiction, the tree warden can make ample provision for their treatment and direct the work intelligently. In most cases the period of time is limited during which the extermination of insect pests may be done most effectively. The treatment of elm-trees for the elm-leaf beetle is a case in point. The insect can be controlled only by spraying, and the time when that may be done most effectively is limited to two or three weeks. When the tree warden knows the total number of elm-trees in his city and the number on each street he can accomplish the most work within the limited time.

The field books and the maps can be used to compute the number of the trees necessary to plant on a street. From the records of the conditions of the trees it will usually be possible to determine what trees are to be cut down. Thus from the descriptions of the trees numbered 10, 19, and 20 on "Shepard Street," it is seen that they are not fit to retain, and they are checked off as trees to be removed.

While the average distance at which certain species are to be planted may be prescribed, the actual spot where the individual specimens are to go cannot be determined from the maps, unless every street obstruction were carefully noted and its position indicated on the map. Such work would entail a great deal of useless labor, for on the average street there are many lamp-posts, fire-hydrants, cross-walks, and water, sewer, and gas connections that are to be avoided. The writer has found from experience that it is better to decide the exact spot where new trees are to be planted while in the field. It usually becomes necessary in many individual instances to increase or diminish the average prescribed distance in order to keep away from points where trees cannot be planted.

After the places for new trees have been marked, their distances apart should be noted in the field book, using a small cross for each tree as shown in the specimen pages. Usually one species is used on a street, and therefore it is not necessary to mark every tree as in the case of existing trees. One record of the species and the date planted may be made in the field book on the first page of the street. A similar record should be entered on the finished office maps.

RECORDS OF NEW TREES

The newly planted trees are plotted on the same maps as the old trees, and are indicated by red circles. These trees are numbered with a new series of numbers, beginning with number 1; but in order not to confuse the new trees with the existing trees a zero "0" is prefixed to the numeral. The beginning of the trees on each street with number "1," or number "01," eliminates the use of large numbers. Each tree is absolutely fixed by the designation of the street and the tree number. A small, inexpensive brass label bearing the tree number might be attached to the guard of each newly planted tree for the purpose of identifying each specimen.

The assigning of numbers to newly planted trees enables the tree warden to keep a record of the behavior of new plantations. Each tree may be recorded on a separate card having the following form:

RECORD OF TREES PLANTED

STREET _____   TREE NUMBER _____

SPECIES _____

WHEN PLANTED _____   SIZE WHEN PLANTED _____

NURSERY WHERE PURCHASED _____

LIFE HISTORY OF TREE _____

_____

_____

_____

_____

_____

Records of the behavior of trees form a fair basis for the judgment of the hardiness of certain species, the quality of stock purchased from various nurseries and the peculiar local conditions affecting tree growth. The causes of the failure of trees should be definitely determined, in order to remedy, if possible, the conditions before new trees are set out, or to improve cultural methods after they are planted. A few years after planting, the life stories of trees might appear as follows: "Planted April, 1905. Died summer 1905, poor underdrainage. Installed drain October, 1905. Replanted spring 1906"; or, "Planted spring 1905. Did not come out in foliage. Dried out in shipment from nursery. Replanted fall 1905"; or, "Planted April, 1905. Foliage dried out summer 1905, failure to water. Replanted spring 1906"; or "Planted April, 1905. Died summer 1909. Dried out. Not enough good soil supplied when planted. Replanted fall 1909"; etc., etc., etc.

OTHER RECORDS

Other forms of office records will readily suggest themselves to the municipal arboriculturist who desires system in his office. When requests are made for attention to trees it is best to keep each item on a separate card, like this:

RECORD OF COMPLAINTS

LOCATION

COMPLAINANT

DATE OF COMPLAINT

REQUEST

DATE OF INSPECTION

CONDITION OF TREES

WORK DONE ON

Daily reports of the work of each gang can be kept on separate cards:

SHADE-TREE COMMISSION—DAILY REPORT

DATE	FOREMAN	
KIND OF WORK	STREETS	NO. OF TREES
TRIMMED		
SPRAYED		
REMOVED		
CEMENTED		
PLANTED		
HOLES DUG		
STAKES DRIVEN		
WATERED		
OTHER WORK		

ASSESSMENT LISTS

When the cost of the trees set out on a street is to be charged to the abutting property-owners the maps, with the newly planted trees carefully located, are absolutely necessary in making up the assessments. When the trees are plotted to scale it is seen just in front of which property they come. Very frequently there are vacant lots on streets planted and there is no way of determining in the field the description of the property. Thus by referring to the map

of "Shepard Street," Fig. 35, it is seen at a glance in front
of which property the new trees come. An assessment
record of the newly planted trees on "Shepard Street" would
then appear as follows:

SHEPARD STREET

Tree Number.	Block Map Number.	Lot Number.	Name of Property-Owner.	No. Feet Frontage	Number of Trees.	Cost.
01	323	119–121	Edward Willis	46	1	$5.00
02–03	323	115–117	Estate Jos. Heller	54	2	10.00
04	322	99–101	Alfred Ward	57	1	5.00
05–06	322	95– 97	Annie Wyman	58	2	10.00
07	322	91– 93	Eastern Realty Co.	55	1	5.00
08–09	322	87– 89	Marcus Rowe	55	2	10.00
010	322	83– 85	Mary Smith	48	1	5.00
011	322	79– 81	Robert Gilbert	50	1	5.00
012	322	75– 77	Robert Mott	52	1	5.00
013–014	316	72– 74	John Williams	60	2	10.00
015	316	76– 78	Joseph Little	50	1	5.00
016	316	80– 82	Peter Sacks	50	1	5.00
017–018	316	84– 88	Walter Jameson	75	2	10.00
019–027	316	90–112	Chas. M. Bingham	310	9	45.00
028–031	317	118–128	Frank J. Hill	150	4	20.00

LABELING TREES

To create an interest in the work of a tree department
and to help the people to become familiar with trees, it is a
good plan to put labels on street-trees, giving the species
and date of planting, in some such form as this:

The Trees on This Street Are

NORWAY MAPLES

They Were Planted by the

SHADE-TREE DEPARTMENT

in the Spring of 1905.

Information about trees spread among the people of a city in an appealing way helps them to realize that hardy trees grow rapidly with proper cultivation, and that it is not necessary to plant trashy, quick-growing trees to secure shade in a few years. Records about trees in the office and outside form interesting commentaries on tree life.

CHAPTER XIII

LEGISLATION

WHILE a number of States have laws regarding the planting and care of street-trees, none are as broad as the provisions of the statutes of New Jersey, Pennsylvania, and Massachusetts. The laws of these States are therefore given in full.

NEW JERSEY

LAWS OF NEW JERSEY

General Public Laws; Session of 1893.

Chapter CCLXXXV.

AN act to provide for the planting and care of shade-trees on the highways of the municipalities of this State.

SECTION 1. BE IT ENACTED *by the Senate and General Assembly of the State of New Jersey,* That in all the municipalities of this State there may be appointed, in the manner hereinafter provided, a commission of three freeholders, who shall serve without compensation, and who shall have the exclusive and absolute control and power to plant, set out, maintain, protect and care for shade-trees in any of the public highways of their respective municipalities, the cost thereof to be borne and paid for in the manner hereinafter directed.

SEC. 2. *And be it enacted,* That it shall be optional with the governing body of any municipality whether this act shall have effect in, and such commissioners shall be appointed in, such municipality; and when any such governing body shall by resolution approve of this act and direct that such commissioners shall be appointed, then, from that time this act and all its provisions shall be in force and apply to such municipality, and such commissioners shall be appointed for terms of three, four, and five years respectively; and on the expiration of any term, the new appointment shall be made for five years, and any vacancy shall be filled for the unexpired term only; and in cities, the said appointments shall be made by the mayor thereof, and in townships by the chairman of the township committee, and in villages and boroughs by the chairman or president of the board of trustees or other governing body.

SEC. 3. *And be it enacted,* That whenever said commissioners shall propose to make any such improvements as setting out or planting any shade-trees, or changing the same in any highways, they shall give notice of such contemplated improvement (specify the streets or portions thereof where such trees are intended to be planted) in one or more newspapers of their said municipality, if there be any newspapers published in said place, for at least two weeks prior to any meeting, in which they shall decide to make such improvement.

SEC. 4. *And be it enacted,* That the cost of planting and transplanting any trees in any highway, and boxes or guards for the protection thereof, when necessary, shall be borne by the real estate in front of which such trees are planted or set out, and the cost thereof as to each tract of real estate shall be certified by said commissioners to the person having charge of the collection of taxes for said municipality; and upon the filing of said certificate, the amount of the cost of said improvement shall be and become a lien upon said lands in front of which the trees were planted or set out, and the said collecting officer shall place the assessment so made against any property in the annual tax bills rendered to owner or owners of such property, and the same shall be collectible in the same manner as the other taxes against said property are collected.

SEC. 5. *And be it enacted,* That the cost and expense of caring for said trees, after being planted or set out, and the expense of publishing said notices, shall be borne and paid by a general tax to be raised by said municipality; said tax shall not exceed the sum of one-tenth of one mill on the dollar annually on all the taxable property of said municipality, and the needed amount shall be each year certified by said commissioners to the assessor, and assessors of said municipality, and be assessed and raised as other taxes.

SEC. 6. *And be it enacted,* That this act shall take effect immediately.

Approved March 28, 1893.

Under Chapter 169, Section 97 of the laws of 1899, this act was repealed in so far as it related to or affected townships.

This act was amended in the years 1905 and 1906 so as to extend the jurisdiction of the shade-tree commissions over the public parks, and to give the commissions the power to pass ordinances for the protection of shade-trees on the public streets and in the public parks.

LAWS OF NEW JERSEY OF 1905.

Chapter 108.

A supplement to an act entitled, "An act to provide for the planting and care of shade-trees on the highways of the municipalities of this state," approved March twenty-eighth, one thousand eight hundred and ninety-three.

BE IT ENACTED *by the Senate and General Assembly of the State of New Jersey:*

SECTION 1. In any municipality which now has or hereafter shall take advantage of the act to which this is a supplement the commission appointed under the provisions thereof shall have exclusive control over the public parks belonging to or under the control of such municipality, or any department in the government thereof, with full power and authority to improve, repair, manage, maintain, and control the same.

SEC. 2. The said commission shall have full power and authority and is hereby empowered to pass, enact, alter, amend, and repeal ordinances for the protection, regulation, and control of such parks, and the trees, flowers, shrubs, statuary therein, and also for the protection, regulation, and control of all shade-trees planted or growing upon the public highways of any such municipality, and to prescribe fines and penalties for the violation thereof and fix the amount of the same; the method now in use for the passing, enacting, altering, amending, and publishing ordinances in said municipality shall be the method used to pass, enact, alter, amend, repeal, and publish the ordinances therein mentioned.

SEC. 3. All moneys collected from fines or penalties for the violation of any ordinances of any such commission, and all moneys collected for assessments made upon the property for the cost of planting and transplanting any trees; and the boxes or guards for the protection thereof in any such city, shall be forthwith paid over to the proper municipal authorities and shall be placed to the credit of the said commission and subject to be drawn upon by the said commission in the manner provided by law for the payments of moneys in any such municipality.

SEC. 4. All acts and parts of acts inconsistent with this act are hereby repealed.

SEC. 5. This act shall take effect immediately.

Approved April 6, 1905.

————

LAWS OF NEW JERSEY OF 1906.

Chapter 186.

A supplement to an act entitled "An act to provide for the planting and care of shade-trees on the highways of the municipalities of this State, approved March twenty-eighth, one thousand eight hundred and ninety-three."

BE IT ENACTED *by the Senate and General Assembly of the State of New Jersey:*

SECTION 1. The said commission may prescribe penalties for the violation of any of their ordinances, and the courts which now or hereafter shall have jurisdiction over actions for the violation of ordinances of the municipality in which said commission has been or shall be appointed shall have jurisdiction in actions for the violation of such ordinances as the said commission shall enact; and said ordinances shall be enforced by like proceedings and processes, and the practise for the enforcement of said ordinances shall be the same as that provided by law for the enforcement of the ordinances of the municipality in which such commission exists.

SEC. 2.   The officers authorized by law to serve and execute processes in the courts, as aforesaid, shall be the officers to serve and execute any process issued out of any court under this act.

SEC. 3.   A copy of any ordinance or ordinances of said commission, certified to under the hand of the clerk, secretary, or president of the said commission, shall be taken in any court of this State as full and legal proof of the existence of such ordinance or ordinances, and that all requirements of law in relation to the ordaining, publishing, and making of the same, so as to make it legal and binding, have been complied with, unless the contrary be shown.

SEC. 4.   This act shall take effect immediately.

Approved May 2, 1906.

———

LAWS OF NEW JERSEY OF 1906.

Chapter 245.

AN act in relation to the control of public parks belonging to or under the control of any municipality of this State or any department in the government thereof:

BE IT ENACTED *by the Senate and General Assembly of the State of New Jersey :*

SECTION 1.   In any municipality which now has or hereafter shall take advantage of an act entitled "An act to provide for the planting and care of shade-trees on the highways of the municipalities of this State, approved March twenty-eighth, one thousand eight hundred and ninety-three," the commission appointed under the provisions of said act shall have exclusive control of the public parks belonging to or under the control of such municipality or any department in the government thereof, with full power and authority to improve, repair, manage, maintain, and control the same.

SEC. 2.   The said commission shall have full power and authority and is hereby empowered to pass, enact, alter, amend, and repeal ordinances for the protection, regulation, and control of such parks and the trees, flowers, shrubs, statuary, and other improvements therein, and to prescribe fines and penalties for the violation thereof and to fix the amount of the same.   The method now or hereafter in use for the passing, enacting, altering, amending, repealing, and publishing ordinances in said municipality shall be the method used to pass, enact, alter, amend, repeal, and publish the ordinances herein mentioned, and said ordinances shall be enforced in the manner provided at the time of said enforcement by law for the enforcement of the ordinances of the commission authorized by the aforesaid act and any amendments or supplements thereof.

SEC. 3.   This act shall take effect immediately.

Approved May 17, 1906.

In the years 1907, 1908, and 1910, the shade-tree law of 1893 was further amended.   Under Chapter 156 of the laws of 1907, Section 1 was amended making it optional with the governing body of any municipality to increase the number of members of the commission to five.   Chapter 151 of the laws of 1908 amended Section 2 so as to make it "optional with the body or board having charge of the finances of any municipality" whether the act of 1893 shall become effective.   Under Chapter 198 of the laws of 1908 and Chapter 167 of the laws of 1910, the law of 1893 was amended as follows: "In any city or town in this State in which a park commission now exists, the governing body invested with the power of adopting the act to which this is a supplement, may, in the resolution adopting said act, provide that the said park commission shall also act as a shade-tree commission; and the act to which this is a supplement, and the amendments thereof and supplements thereto, shall take effect in said city or town, except that no independent shade-tree commission shall be appointed."

PENNSYLVANIA

LAWS OF PENNSYLVANIA

Session of 1907

AN act to provide for the planting and care of shade-trees, on highways of townships of the first class, boroughs, and cities of the Commonwealth of Pennsylvania, and providing for the cost thereof.

SECTION 1. BE IT ENACTED, *etc.,* That in townships of the first class, boroughs, and cities of Commonwealth of Pennsylvania there may be appointed, in the manner hereinafter provided, a Commission of three freeholders, to be known and designated as the Shade-Tree Commission of said township, borough, or city, who shall serve without compensation, and who shall have exclusive and absolute custody and control of, and power to plant, set out, remove, maintain, protect, and care for shade-trees, on any of the public highways of the said townships, boroughs, and cities, the cost thereof to be provided for in the manner hereinafter stated: *Provided,* That in townships, boroughs, or cities in which a Commission for the care of public parks shall have been created, said Commission shall, upon the acceptance of this act as provided in section two, be charged with the duties of the Commission as above provided, and shall, for that purpose, be possessed of all the powers herein mentioned and granted.

SEC. 2. The commissioners of any township of the first class, or the council of any borough or city, in case of the commissioners, or by joint resolution in the case of the councils,

accept the provisions of this act; and when such majority vote
or joint resolution shall have been duly passed and approved, and
such Shade-Tree Commissioners appointed, or, in their stead, the
duties and powers herein provided have been devolved upon an
existing park commission, then, from that time and in that
event, this act and all its provisions shall be in full force and
application in such township of the first class, borough, or city,
so accepting; and such commissioners shall be appointed, for
terms of three, four, and five years, respectively, and, on the
expiration of any term, the new appointment shall be for five
years, and any vacancies shall be filled for the unexpired term
only; and in townships of the first class the said appointment
shall be made by the commissioners thereof; and in boroughs, by
the chief burgess, and in cities, by the mayor thereof: *Provided,*
That in cities where a Commission exists for the care of public
parks, the term and appointment of such Commission shall not
be changed by this act, but shall be and remain as provided by
the act of Assembly, and by the ordinance of councils creating
such Commission for the care and maintenance of public parks.
And such Shade-Tree Commission shall, twice in every year,
report in full its transactions and expenditures for the municipal
fiscal year then last ended, to the authority under and by which
it was appointed: *Provided,* That an existing park commission,
acting under this enactment, may embody its report in its regular report to the councils, as by law or ordinance provided.

SEC. 3.   That when such Shade-Tree Commissioners, or Park
Commissioners so acting, shall propose the setting out or planting or removing of any shade-trees, or the material changing of
the same in any highway, they shall give public notice of the
time and place appointed for the meeting at which such contemplated work is to be considered, specifying in detail the highways, or portion thereof, upon which trees are proposed to be
planted, removed, or changed, in one or more—not exceeding
two in all—of the newspapers published in said township, borough, or city once each week for at least two weeks prior to the
date of said meeting.

SEC. 4.   The cost of planting, transplanting, or removing any trees in any highway, and of suitable guards, curbing, or grating for the protection thereof when necessary, and of the proper replacing of any pavement or sidewalk necessarily disturbed in the doing of such work, shall be borne by the owner of the real estate in front of which such trees are planted, set out, or removed; and the cost thereof as to each tract of real estate shall be certified by the commissioners to the township commissioners, or to the presidents of the councils in boroughs and cities, and also to the person having charge of the collection of taxes, for the said township, borough, or city; and upon the filing of said certificates, the amount of the cost of such improvements, of which notice shall also be given to each property-owner involved, accompanied with a copy of the aforesaid certificate, together with a notice of the time and place for payment, shall be and become a lien upon said real estate, in front of which said trees have been planted, set out, or removed; said lien to be collectible, if not paid in accordance with notice as herein provided, in the same manner as other liens for taxes are now collectible against the property involved.

SEC. 5.   The cost and expense of caring for said trees after having been planted or set out, and the expense of publishing the notices provided for in section three, shall be borne and paid for by a general tax, to be levied annually in the manner that taxes for township, borough, and city purposes are now levied in such townships of the first class, boroughs, or cities; such tax not to exceed the sum of one-tenth of one mill on the dollar on the assessed valuation of the property in such townships of the first class, boroughs, or cities; and the needed amount shall each year, in due time be certified by the Shade-Tree Commissioners to the proper authorities charged with the assessment of taxes in said townships, boroughs, or cities, to be assessed and paid, as other taxes are assessed and paid, and to be drawn against as required by said commissioners, in the same manner as moneys appropriated for township, borough, or city purposes are now drawn against in said townships, boroughs, or cities; *Provided,* That the commissioners of any township of the first class, and the councils of any borough or city, accepting the provisions of this act, may provide for the expense of the maintenance of trees on highways, in accordance with the provisions of this section by actual appropriation, equal to the amount certified to be required by the said Commission, in lieu of the specific assessment above authorized.

SEC. 6.   The Commission, under which the provisions of this act shall be carried out, in any township of the first class, borough, or city, shall have power to employ and pay such superintendents, engineers, foresters, tree-wardens, or other assistants, as the proper performance of the duties devolving upon it shall require; and to make, publish, and enforce regulations for the care of, and to prevent injury to the trees, on the highways of any township, borough, or city accepting the provisions of this act; and to assess suitable fines and penalties for violations of this act, provided such regulations shall have been published at least twice in one or more, not exceeding two, newspapers of the township, borough, or city involved, after having been submitted to and being approved by the commissioners of the township of the first class, or the councils of the borough or city affected; and such fines and penalties, so assessed for violations of this act, shall become liens upon the real property of the offender, and be collectible by the constituted authorities as liens for taxes upon real property are now collected.

SEC. 7.   All the moneys due and collected from fines or penalties or assessments, in consequence of the acts of said Shade-Tree Commission in enforcing this act, shall be paid to the treasurers of the townships, boroughs, and cities accepting its provisions, and shall be placed to the credit of said Commission, subject to be drawn upon by the said Commission for the purposes of this act.

SEC. 8.   All acts and parts of acts inconsistent with this act are hereby repealed.

SEC. 9.   This act shall take effect immediately; but its provisions shall not be and become binding upon any township, borough, or city until it has been duly accepted, as provided in section two.

Approved.—The 31st day of May, A.D. 1907.

MASSACHUSETTS

The act originally known as the "Tree Warden Act" is as follows:

AN ACT TO CODIFY AND AMEND THE LAWS RELATIVE TO THE PRESERVATION OF TREES.

(Acts of 1899, Chapter 330.)

BE IT ENACTED, *etc., as follows:*

SECTION 1. Every town shall at its annual meeting for the election of town officers elect a tree warden, who shall serve for one year and until his successor is elected and qualified. He may appoint such number of deputy tree wardens as he deems expedient, and may at any time remove them from office. He and his deputies shall receive such compensation for their services as the town may determine, and, in default of such determination, as the selectmen may prescribe. He shall have the care and control of all public shade-trees in the town, except those in public parks or open places under the jurisdiction of park commissioners, and of these also he shall take the care and control if so requested in writing by the park commissioners. He shall expend all funds appropriated for the setting out and maintenance of such trees. He may prescribe such regulations for the care and preservation of such trees, enforced by suitable fines and forfeitures, not exceeding twenty dollars in any one case, as he may deem just and expedient; and such regulations, when approved by the selectmen and posted in two or more public places in the town, shall have the force and effect of town by-laws. It shall be his duty to enforce all provisions of law for the preservation of such trees.

SEC. 2. Towns may appropriate annually a sum of money, not exceeding in the aggregate fifty cents for each of its ratable polls in the preceding year, to be expended by the tree warden in planting shade-trees in the public ways, or, if he deems it expedient, upon adjoining land, at a distance not exceeding twenty feet from said public ways, for the purpose of shading or ornamenting the same: *provided, however,* that the written consent of the owner of such land shall first be obtained. All shade-trees within the limits of any public way shall be deemed public shade-trees.

SEC. 3. Whoever, other than a tree warden or his deputy, desires the cutting or removal, in whole or in part, of any public shade-tree, may apply to the tree warden, who shall give a public hearing upon the application at some suitable time and place, after duly posting notices of the hearing in two or more public places in the town, and also upon the said tree: *provided, however,* that the warden may, if he deems it expedient, grant permission for such cutting or removal, without calling a hearing, if the tree in question is on a public way outside of the residential part of the town, the limits of such residential part to be determined by the selectmen. No tree within such residential part shall be cut by the tree warden, except to trim it, or removed by him without a hearing as aforesaid; but in all cases the decision of the tree warden shall be final.

SEC. 4. Towns may annually raise and appropriate such sum of money as they deem necessary, to be expended under the direction of the tree warden in exterminating insect pests within the limits of their public ways and places, and in the removal from said public ways and places of all trees and other plants upon which such pests naturally breed: *provided, however,* that where an owner or lessee of real estate shall, to the satisfaction of the tree warden, annually exterminate all insect pests upon the trees and other plants within the limits of any public way or place abutting on said real estate, such trees and plants shall be exempt from the provisions of this section.

SEC. 5. Whoever affixes to any tree in a public way or place a play-bill, picture, announcement, notice, advertisement, or other thing, whether in writing or otherwise, or cuts, paints, or marks such tree, except for the purpose of protecting it and under a written permit from the tree warden, shall be punished by a fine not exceeding fifty dollars for each offence.

SEC. 6. Whoever wantonly injures, defaces, breaks, or destroys an ornamental or shade tree within the limits of any public way or place shall forfeit not less than five nor more than one hundred dollars, to be recovered by complaint, one-half to the complainant and the other half to the use of the town.

SEC. 7.   Whoever negligently or carelessly suffers a horse or other beast driven by or for him, or a beast belonging to him and lawfully in a public way or place, to break down, injure, or destroy a shade or ornamental tree within the limits of said public way or place, or whoever negligently or wilfully by any other means breaks down, injures, or destroys any such tree, shall be liable to the penalties prescribed in the foregoing section, and shall in addition be liable for all damages caused thereby.

SEC. 8.   It shall be the duty of the tree warden to enforce the provisions of the preceding sections.   (Approved May 4, 1899.)

The above law of Massachusetts has never been repealed, but it has been several times amended, mainly in the direction of extending and more accurately defining the duties and powers of shade-tree officials.

In 1902 a general revision of the State laws was made by the legislature, and the principal provisions of Chap. 330, of the Acts of 1899, were embodied in Chap. 53 of the Revised Laws, although several provisions of the original chapter were distributed in other places.   This arrangement has made it somewhat difficult to refer to the laws relating to shade-trees, and has led the Massachusetts Forestry Association to issue, from time to time, compilations of the law brought up to date.

By Chap. 363, of the Acts of 1910, the "Tree Warden Act" has been extended in practically all of its provisions, except that requiring the election of a tree warden, to the cities of Massachusetts.

The extensions of the "Tree Warden Act," and the amendments thereto, as regards the authority of city and town officers, are embodied in the following:

R. L., Ch. 53, Sections 6 to 11 (as amended by Acts of 1908, ch. 296), including the old spike provision. Repealed by Acts of 1910, ch. 363, which follows.

Acts of 1910, Ch. 363, Section 1.   The powers and duties conferred upon tree wardens in towns by Section 12 and 13 of Chapter 53 of the Revised Laws, as amended by Chapter 296 of the Acts of 1908, are hereby conferred upon officials now charged with the care of shade-trees within the limits of the highway in cities, by the charters of the said cities, by other legislative enactment or ordinances of the city governments of said cities, and upon such officials as the city governments shall hereafter designate to have charge of said shade-trees where it is within their powers to transfer such duties, by ordinance or otherwise.

SEC. 2.   Sections 6, 7, 8, 9, 10 and 11 of Chapter 53 of the Revised Laws are hereby repealed.

R. L., Ch. 11, Section 334.   Every town at its annual meeting shall in every year, except as is otherwise provided in the following section and in Sections 339 and 341, choose from the inhabitants thereof the following named town officers, who shall serve during the year: . . . . a tree warden.

R. L., Ch. 53, Section 12 (as amended by Chap. 296, Acts of 1908, Section 2, and Chap. 321, Acts of 1910).   The tree warden may appoint and remove deputy tree wardens.   He and they shall receive such compensation as the town determines, or, in default thereof, as the selectmen allow.   He shall have the care and control of all public shade-trees in the town, except those in public parks or open places under the jurisdiction of the park commissioners, and of those, if so requested in writing by the park commissioners, and shall enforce all the provisions of law for the preservation of such trees. He shall expend all money appropriated for the setting out and maintenance of such trees, but no trees shall be planted within the limits of a public way without the approval of the tree warden, and until a location therefor has been obtained from the selectmen, or from the road commissioners where authority has been vested in them.   Regulations for the care and preservation of public shade-trees made by him,

approved by the selectmen and posted in two or more public
places, imposing fines and forfeitures of not more than twenty
dollars in any one case, shall have the force and effect of town
by-laws. All shade-trees within or on the limits of a public way
shall be public shade-trees; and when it appears in any civil
proceeding under process of law where the ownership of or rights
in the tree are material to the issue, that from length of time or
otherwise, the boundaries of the highway cannot be made certain
by the records or by monuments, and for that reason it is doubt-
ful whether the tree was within or without the limits of the highway, it shall be taken to have been within the limits of the highway until the contrary is shown.

SEC. 13 (*as amended by Chap. 296, Acts of 1908, Section 3*).
Public shade-trees shall not be cut or removed, in whole or in
part, except by the tree warden or his deputy, or by a person
holding a license so to do from the tree warden, nor shall they
be removed by the tree warden or his deputy or other person
without public hearing at a suitable time and place, after notice
thereof posted in two or more public places in the town and upon
the tree and after authority granted by the tree warden therefor.
Whoever violates the provisions of this section shall forfeit not
less than five nor more than one hundred dollars to the use of
the town.

Acts of 1908, Chap. 296, Section 4. Nothing in this act shall
be construed as applying to any highway now or hereafter within
the jurisdiction of the state highway commission.

R. L., Ch. 25, Section 15. It (a town) may at legal meetings
appropriate money for the following purposes: . . . . . For
planting shade-trees in the public ways or, at the discretion of
the tree warden and with the written consent of the owner
thereof, upon land adjoining such ways at not more than twenty
feet from the way for the purpose of shading or ornamenting the
way, an amount not exceeding fifty cents for each of its ratable
polls in the preceding year.

SEC. 16. Towns may appropriate money to be expended under
the direction of the tree warden for exterminating insect pests in

the public ways and places, and for removing therefrom trees and
plants upon which such insects naturally breed, except trees and
plants from which the owner or lessee of land abutting on said
public way or place annually exterminates all such insect pests
to the satisfaction of the tree warden.

ORDINANCES

The State laws of New Jersey, Pennsylvania, and Massachusetts leave each town and city free to supplement the
statutes by local ordinances. The provisions of such ordinances are of course varied by special local conditions; but
the general points to be covered by them will be indicated
in the sections of the East Orange Shade-Tree Ordinance:

AN ORDINANCE relating to the planting, protection, regulation, and control of shade-trees planted or growing upon the
public highways of the city of East Orange, Essex County, New
Jersey.

Be it ordained by the Shade-Tree Commission of the City of
East Orange, N. J., as follows:

SECTION 1. No individual or officer or employee of a corporation shall, without the written permit of the Shade-Tree Commission, cut, prune, break, climb, injure, or remove any living
tree in a public highway; or cut, disturb, or interfere in any way
with the roots of any tree on a public highway; or spray with
any chemicals or insecticides any tree in a public highway; or
place any rope, sign, poster, or other fixture on a tree or guard
in a public highway; or injure, misuse, or remove any device
placed to protect such tree on a public highway.

SEC. 2. No shade or ornamental tree or shrub shall be
planted in any of the public highways of the City of East Orange
until such tree or shrub shall have first been approved and the
place where it is to be planted designated by the Shade-Tree
Commission, and a permit granted therefor.

SEC. 3. No person shall fasten a horse or other animal to a
tree in a public highway in the City of East Orange, nor cause a

horse or other animal to stand so that said horse or animal can injure such a tree.

SEC. 4.   No person shall, without the written permit of the Shade-Tree Commission, place or hereafter maintain upon the ground in a public highway, stone, cement, or other substance which shall impede the free passage of water and air to the roots of any tree in such highway, without leaving an open space of ground outside of the trunk of said tree in area not less than four feet square.

SEC. 5.   In the erection or repair of any building or structure the owner thereof shall place such guards around all nearby trees on the public highway as shall effectually prevent injury to them.

SEC. 6.   No person shall pour salt water upon any public highway in such a way as to injure any tree planted or growing thereon.

SEC. 7.   No person shall, without the written permit of the Shade-Tree Commission, attach any electric wire, insulator, or any device for the holding of an electric wire to any tree growing or planted upon any public highway of the City of East Orange.

SEC. 8.   Every person or corporation having any wire or wires charged with electricity running through a public highway, shall securely fasten such wire or wires so that they shall not come in contact with any tree therein.

SEC. 9.   Every person or corporation having any wire or wires charged with electricity running through a public highway, shall temporarily remove any such wire or wires or the electricity therefrom when it shall be necessary, in order to take down or prune any trees growing in a public highway, within twenty-four hours after the service upon the owner of said wire or wires, or his agent, of a written notice to remove said wire or wires or the electricity therefrom, signed by two members of the Shade-Tree Commission, or its secretary, upon the order of such Commission.

SEC. 10.   No person or corporation shall prevent, delay, or interfere with the Shade-Tree Commission or its employees, in the planting, pruning, spraying, or removing of a tree on a public highway, or in the removal of stone, cement, or other substance about the trunk of a tree.

SEC. 11. Every repeated violation by the same person of any provision of this ordinance, or the continuation of the violation of any of its provisions on any day or days succeeding the first violation thereof, shall constitute an additional violation of such provision.

SEC. 12. Any person violating any of the provisions of this ordinance shall, upon conviction thereof, forfeit and pay a penalty of ten dollars for each offence.

SEC. 13. This ordinance shall take effect immediately.

Adopted May 13, 1907.

Sample pages from actual field book, for enumerating street trees.

Blank field books may be obtained from the publishers.

Field books 4½ inches x 7¾ inches 160 pages.

Prices: $1.25 net each, and $12.00 net in lots of one dozen.

Tree No.	Species	Diameter	Condition	Remarks
		Street ---- Shepard Street ---- Date ---- Oct. 18, 1904 ---		
1	Norway Maple	5"	Good	
2	White Maple	16"	"	
3	White Maple	12"	Medium	Cavity in trunk
4	Sugar Maple	14"	Good	
5	Norway Maple	10"	Good	
6	Red Maple	16"	Medium	Branch decayed
7	Red Maple	14"	Good	
8	White Elm	10"	Good	
9	" "	12"	"	
10	White Maple	10"	Bad	Cavity - cannot be repaired
19	Red Maple	14"	"	Nearly dead
20	" "	16"	"	Trunk rotted
21	White Maple	14"	Good	
22	" "	15"	"	
23	Red Maple	7"	"	
24	" "	7"	"	
25	" "	9"	Medium	Cavity
26	" "	8"	Good	
27	" "	8"	Good	
28	" "	8"	"	
				Planted Norway Maples April, 1905

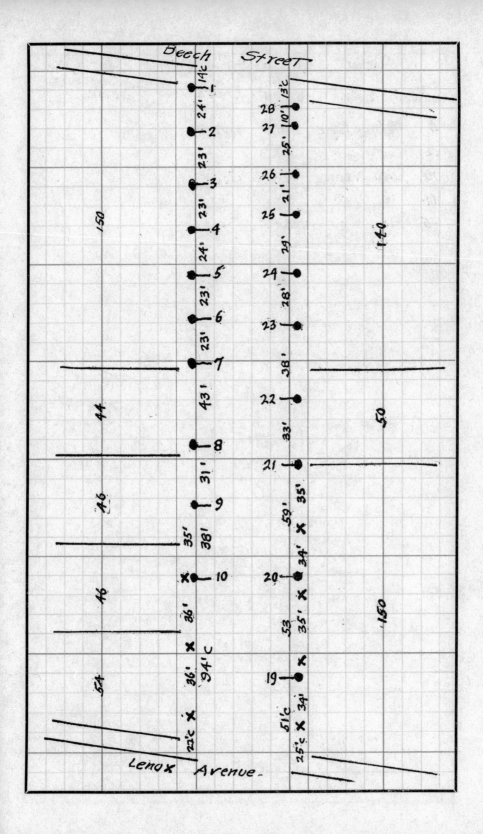

Tree No.	Species	Diameter	Condition	Remarks
11	Norway Maple	10"	Good	
12	" "	12"	"	
13	Red Maple	4"	Good	
14	" "	6"	"	
15	" "	6"	"	

Street____Shepard Street____Date____Oct. 18, 1904.___

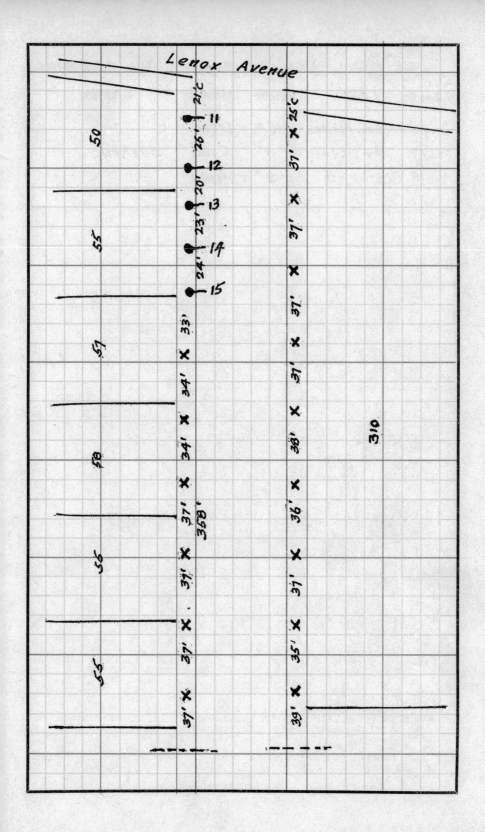

| Street | | Shepard Street | | Date | Oct. 18, 1904 |
Tree No.	Species	Diameter	Condition	Remarks
16	Am. Linden	6"	Good	
17	Am. Elm	8"	Good	Barked
18	" "	9"	Good	

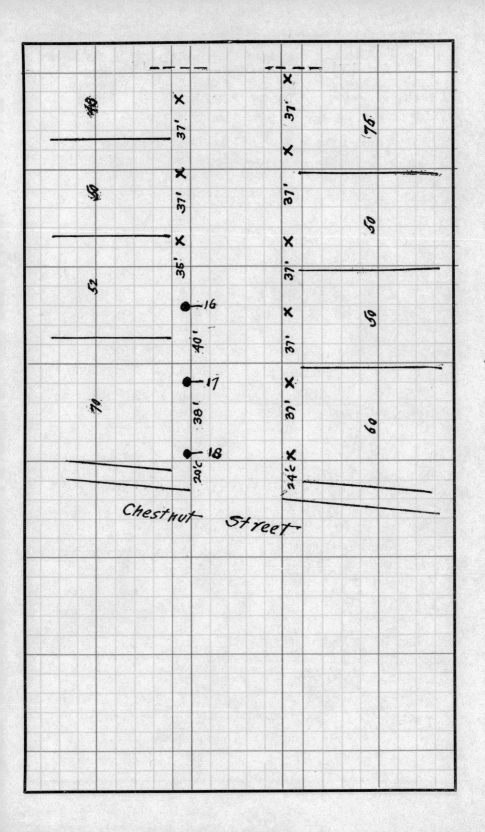

Tree No.	Street		Date	
	Species	Diameter	Condition	Remarks

INDEX

Numbers refer to pages. Illustrations are indicated by an asterisk after page number.

277

BOOKS

ON

FORESTRY

PUBLISHED BY

JOHN WILEY & SONS, Inc.

NEW YORK

Books on Forestry

Forest Physiography— Physiography of the United States and Principles of Soils in Relation to Forestry.

By ISAIAH BOWMAN, Ph.D., Director, American Geographical Society. xii+759 pages. 6 by 9. 292 figures and 6 plates, including a New Geologic Map of North America, in colors. Cloth...............net, **$5.00**

A book on physiography for students of forestry, and also a work which historians and economists will find of value.

Elements of Forestry.

By FREDERICK FRANKLIN MOON, B.A., M.F., Dean, and NELSON COURTLANDT BROWN, B.A., M.F., Professor of Forest Utilization, The New York State College of Forestry, Syracuse University. Second Edition, Revised and Rewritten. xvii+403 pages. 5¼ by 8. 71 figures. Cloth. net, **$3.50**

A textbook of broad scope, containing general information on all phases of the subject.

Forest Products; Their Manufacture and Use.

By NELSON COURTLANDT BROWN, B.A., M.F., Dean, The New York State College of Forestry, Syracuse University. xix+471 pages. 6 by 9. 120 figures. Cloth **$4.00**

A book for lumbermen, manufacturers, users and importers of forest products, foresters, and students in professional schools of forestry.

The American Lumber Industry.

By NELSON COURTLANDT BROWN. xiv+279 pages. 6 by 9. 39 figures. Cloth ....net, **$3.00**

Embracing the principal features of the resources, production, distribution and utilization of lumber in the United States.

Logging— The Principles and General Methods of Operation in the United States.

By RALPH CLEMENT BRYANT, F.E., M.A., Manufacturers' Association Professor of Lumbering, Yale University. Second Edition, Thoroughly Revised and Reset. xiii+556 pages. 6 by 9. 165 figures. Cloth. net, **$4.50**

Discusses at length the chief facilities and methods for the movement of the timber from the stump to the manufacturing plant.

Lumber: Its Manufacture and Distribution.

By RALPH CLEMENT BRYANT. xxi+539 pages. 6 by 9. 156 figures. Cloth ....net, **$4.50**

The only textbook on lumber manufacture and distribution now available in any language.

Forest Valuation.

By HERMAN HAUPT CHAPMAN, M.F., Harriman Professor of Forest Management, Yale University Forest School. xvi+310 pages. 6 by 9. Cloth ....net, **$3.00**

Treats the subject in a manner that may be readily grasped by the average reader, without previous preparation or study.

Forest Mensuration.

By HERMAN HAUPT CHAPMAN, M.F. Second Edition, Revised. xvii+
557 pages. 6 by 9. 88 figures. Cloth........................net, **$5.00**

A thorough discussion of the measurement of the volume of felled timber,
in the forms of logs or other products, of the measurement of the volume
of standing timber, and of the growth of trees, stands of timber and forests.

Farm Forestry.

By JOHN ARDEN FERGUSON, A.M., M.F., Professor of Forestry at The
Pennsylvania State College. viii+241 pages. 5¼ by 8. Illustrated.
Cloth ....net, **$2.00**

This book brings together in available form ideas and principles relating to
the care and management of the farm woodlot and the utilization of the
products of the woodlot.

The Principles of Handling Woodlands.

By HENRY SOLON GRAVES, M.A., Dean of the School of Forestry, Yale
University, Sterling Professor of Forestry. xxi+325 pages. 5¼ by 8.
63 figures. Cloth ....net, **$2.50**

Takes up the cutting of mature stands of timber and their replacement by
new growth; cuttings in immature stands, and forest protection with reference to forest fires.

Principles of American Forestry.

By SAMUEL B. GREEN, Late Professor of Horticulture and Forestry,
University of Minnesota. xiii+334 pages. 5 by 7¼. 73 figures. Cloth,
$2.00

A book for the general reader who wishes to secure a general idea of the
subject of forestry in North America.

Manual of Forestry for the Northeastern United States.

Being Part I of "Forestry in New England," Revised.

By RALPH CHIPMAN HAWLEY, M.F., Professor of Forestry, Yale University, and AUSTIN FOSTER HAWES, M.F., State Forester of Connecticut.
xii+281 pages. 6 by 9. 65 figures. Cloth.................net, **$3.50**

Furnishes the woodland owner with a brief survey of the whole field of
forestry.

The Practice of Silviculture.

With Particular Reference to Its Application in the United States. By
RALPH CHIPMAN HAWLEY. xi + 353 pages. 5¼ by 8. 82 figures.
Cloth ....net, **$4.00**

A new textbook, presenting the subject from the standpoint of the teacher
and covering a field heretofore unfilled.

The Development of Forest Law in America.

By J. P KINNEY, A.B., LL.B., M.F., Chief Supervisor of Forests, United
States Indian Service. xxxix+254 pages. 6 by 9. Cloth.....net, **$2.50**

A logical presentation of the chronological development of legislation in
this field.

The Essentials of American Timber Law.

By J. P KINNEY, A.B., LL.B., M.F. xxix+279 pages. 6 by 9. Cloth, net, **$3.00**

Gives the existing law regarding trees and their products as property. A book for both foresters and lawyers.
Both books ordered at one time................................net **$5.00**

Studies of Trees.

By J. J. LEVISON, B.A., M.F., formerly Lecturer on Ornamental and Shade Trees, Yale University Forest School. x+253 pages. 5¼ by 8. 155 half-tone figures. Cloth...................................net, **$2.00**

Takes up in a brief and not too technical way the most important facts concerning the identification, structure and uses of our more common trees, considering their habits, enemies and care.

(Also issued in loose-leaf form. Complete set of 20 pamphlets, 8 by 10½, **$1.00** net. Cloth binder, sold separately, **50** cents net.)

Forest Management.

By A. B. RECKNAGEL, B.A., M.F., Professor of Forest Management and Utilization, and JOHN BENTLEY, JR., B.S., M.F., Professor of Forest Engineering, Cornell University. xiii+267 pages. 6 by 9. 26 figures. Cloth ....net, **$2.50**

Treats the subjects, forest mensuration, forest organization, forest finance, and forest administration in such a manner as to be readily understood and used by the layman timber owner and manager.

The Theory and Practice of Working Plans (Forest Organization).

By A. B. RECKNAGEL, B.A., M.F. Second Edition, Thoroughly Revised. xiv+265 pages. 6 by 9. Illustrated. Cloth ....net, **$2.50**

A book of value to the practicing forester, as well as to the student. The best of European methods are presented, adapted to the needs of American forestry.

Identification of the Economic Woods of the United States.

Including a Discussion of the Structural and Physical Properties of Wood. Second Edition, Revised and Enlarged.

By SAMUEL J. RECORD, M.A., M.F., Professor of Forest Products, Yale University. ix+157 pages. 6 by 9. 15 figures and 6 full-page half-tone plates. Cloth ....net, **$2.50**

An efficient aid in the study and identification of wood. The new edition brings the work right up to date in every respect.

The Mechanical Properties of Wood.

Including a Discussion of the Factors Affecting the Mechanical Properties, and Methods of Timber Testing.

By SAMUEL J. RECORD, M.A., M.F. xi+165 pages. 6 by 9. 51 figures. Cloth ....net, **$2.50**

All unnecessary technical language and descriptions have been avoided, making the subject-matter readily available to everyone interested in wood.

Range and Pasture Management.

By ARTHUR W. SAMPSON, M.A., Ph.D., Associate Professor of Range Management and Forest Ecology, University of California. xix+421 pages. 6 by 9. 130 figures, 1 plate showing stock-poisoning plants in natural colors. Cloth ....net, **$4.00**

Provides systematic instruction for those who desire a practical working knowledge of the subject, as well as for those who wish to follow technical grazing work as a profession and fit themselves for such positions as those offered by the United States Forest Service.

Livestock Husbandry on Range and Pasture.

By ARTHUR W. SAMPSON. (In Preparation.)

Devoted to a discussion of the management of range and pasture livestock.

Native American Forage Plants.

By ARTHUR W. SAMPSON, M.A., Ph.D. 435 pages. 6 by 9. 199 figures. Colored Frontispiece showing an idealized composite range. Cloth, net, **$5.00**

Treats in detail all important native forage grasses and broad-leaved plants; pasture values, natural history, growth requirements and life processes of vegetation as related to forage production; and pastural botany.

Shade-Trees in Towns and Cities.

By WILLIAM SOLOTAROFF, B.S., Late Secretary and Superintendent of the Shade-Tree Commission of East Orange, N. J. xviii+287 pages. 6 by 9. 46 full-page plates and 35 figures in the text. Cloth........net, **$3.50**

Takes up the questions of the selection, planting and care of trees as applied to the art of street decoration; their diseases and remedies; their municipal control and supervision.

Field Book for Street-Tree Mapping.

By WILLIAM SOLOTAROFF, B.S. 160 pages. 4½ by 7¾. Each, **$1.25** net. One dozen ....net, **$12.00**

Blank field books for enumerating street-trees when taking a tree census.

Handbook for Rangers and Woodsmen.

By JAY L. B. TAYLOR, formerly Forest Ranger, United States Forest Service. ix+420 pages. 4¼ by 6¾. 236 figures. Flexible binding. net, **$3.00**

A guide for inexperienced men in woods work, and for others whose work or recreation takes them into rough and unsettled regions.

Seeding and Planting in the Practice of Forestry.

By JAMES W. TOUMEY, M.S., M.A., Morris K. Jesup Professor of Silviculture, Yale School of Forestry. xxxvi+455 pages. 6 by 9. 140 figures. Cloth ....net, **$4.00**

A manual for the guidance of forestry students, foresters, nurserymen, forest owners, and farmers.

Handbook of Field and Office Problems in Forest Mensuration.

By HUGO WINKENWERDER, Dean, College of Forestry, University of Washington, and ELIAS T. CLARK, Professor of Forestry, University of Washington. ix+133 pages. 5 by 7½. Flexible binding....net, **$2.00**

A series of carefully selected type exercises prepared as an aid to the laboratory instruction in forest mensuration, which may be used as practical illustrations to supplement recitation and textbook work.

The Valuation of American Timberlands.

By K. W. WOODWARD, Professor of Forestry, New Hampshire State College. vii+253 pages. 6 by 9. 13 figures. Cloth............net, **$3.00**

This book supplies valuable information needed by the investor, timber cruiser and student of forestry. It gives for the continental United States and its outlying territories, Hawaii and the Canal Zone excepted, the principal facts regarding the timber resources.

French Forests and Forestry—Tunisia, Algeria, Corsica. With a Translation of the Algerian Code of 1903.

By THEODORE S. WOOLSEY, JR., M.F., Executive Member of the Inter-allied War Timber Committee, 1917-1919, Paris, France; formerly Lecturer, Yale Forest School. xv+238 pages. 6 by 9. Illustrated. Cloth.
net, **$3.00**

The results of a study of the more important phases of forest practice in Corsica, Algeria, and Tunisia, setting forth the essentials of method which may be applied directly in the United States.

Studies in French Forestry.

By THEODORE S. WOOLSEY, JR. Two chapters by WILLIAM B. GREELEY, formerly Chief of the Forestry Section, Engineers, A.E.F., Tours, France, and now Chief Forester, U. S. Forest Service. vii+550 pages. 6 by 9. Profusely illustrated ....net, **$6.00**

This general book on French forestry is of interest to students, practicing foresters, lumbermen, estate owners, and all members of the 10th and 20th Engineers (Forestry) A. E. F.

Forest Protection.

By DAVID T. MASON, Forest Engineer. (In Preparation.)

Shows how the facts and principles developed by entomologists, pathologists, and others may be applied in a businesslike way to the protection of forests.